Stock Market Investing for Beginners:

And Intermediate. Learn to Generate Passive Income with Investing, Stock Trading, Day Trading Stock. Useful for Cryptocurrency. Great to Listen in a Car!

Table of Contents

Introduction

Congratulations on downloading *Stock Market Investing for Beginners: And Intermediate* and thank you for doing so. While the first book in this series helped you grow accustomed to the ins and outs of the stock market, this book aims to help you take things to the next level by providing you with a greater variety of ways to interact with the stock market than ever before.

The following chapters will discuss everything you need to know to take your understanding of ways to profit from stocks to the next level, starting with a breakdown of the current market climate and what to expect from 2019. Next, you will learn about value and growth investing and why one of them is likely the right choice for you.

While you may have spent much of your time up to this point with relatively passive strategies to profit from the stock market, this book will help move you towards some more active alternatives. To wit, you will find chapters on cloud pattern trading and price action trading two popular trading strategies based on technical analysis. From there, you will find chapters outlining various other types of stock investments and starter strategies to try including dividend stocks, penny stocks, options and more. Finally, you will a chapter dedicated to some of the master of stock investing and the tactics they use to be successful as well as a chapter dedicated to ensuring you remain on the right side of the IRS and pay your taxes correctly.

With so many choices out there when it comes to consuming this type of content, it is appreciated that you've chosen this one. Plenty of care and effort went into ensuring it contains as many interesting and useful tidbits as possible, please enjoy!

Chapter 1: Current Climate

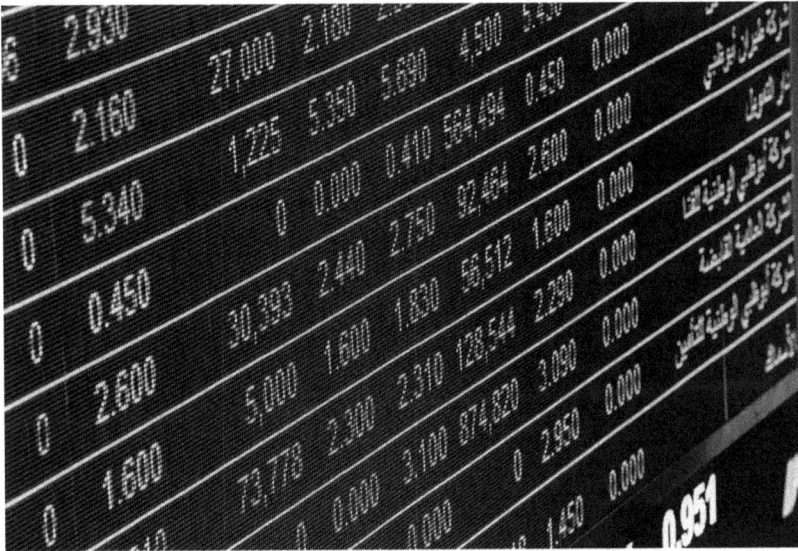

While 2018 ended up being a mixed bag for the stock market, the early predictions for 2019 are muddy at best. The hope on Wall Street is that the underlying economy of the US will remain sound and the current round of selling will fizzle out and that stocks across all industry can resume a steady climb. However, as the first quarter of the year continues to mature, there continues to be a risk that the worst annual decline in a decade could kick in, bringing something entirely more sinister along with it.

The fact of the matter is that all of the forces that caused the S&P 500 to drop more than five percent last year are still in place and while the economy is doing well over all, it is clear to everyone that it is nowhere near as strong as it once was. As there are a variety of important scenarios (discussed below) that can all be used to gauge the seriousness of the potential decline, it is entirely possible the market will enter a tumultuous period where it is bouncing back and forth with each new turn of events.

Last year was a reminder of how unpredictable stock markets can be. In January, with corporate tax cuts in place, the outlook for the market in the United States was great. And stocks did hit a record high in September, with Apple and Amazon becoming the first publicly traded American companies to be valued at more than $1 trillion. But 2018 was also turbulent, with markets falling sharply in February and again at the end of the year.

Furthermore, the S&P 500 nearly hit a milestone of another sort, narrowly avoiding seeing a 20 percent drop from the previous high and ushering in a bear market. In fact, the index ended the year down nearly 15 percent from its high and a bear market could likely return if enough stocks see a decline similar to what occurred in the market at the end of 2018. If this happens then the pessimism that has been hovering around the market could return and spread to other sectors of the economy as companies stop taking risks for fear of hardship that may or may not arrive. What follows are a number of important to keep an eye on in the coming months to help you determine where the market is headed.

Interest rates negatively affected by borrowing costs: Rising expectations about ever-increasing interest rates clearly weighed on stock prices through 2018. In fact, as the economy hummed along, the Fed increased its target rate four times last year, pushing up borrowing costs as a result. The yield seen on a 10-year treasury note, which is how debt for home mortgages is determined, climbed to its highest levels since 2011 at one point. As there is no end in sight for these rising borrowing costs, it is not a question of if the economy will suffer but when. If relief isn't found in this arena soon it could very well cause a recession.

The only thing that will ease off of this course of action is more data on the state of the economy as a whole as if investors can see that the economy is growing, then fears over a potential recession will fade away. If this doesn't happen then you can expect noticeable movement in the market around every monetary policy meeting for the entire year.

Global growth has led to a decrease in commodity prices: The biggest impact of the latest trade war is the negative impact it is having on overseas economies. The European Union, Japan and China all showed signs of slowing in the second half of 2018 and indicators like copper and oil prices are both indicating that things will get worse before it gets better. Ideally, growth will accelerate if beneficial trade agreements are signed in 2019, but it is possible the problems will continue to go deeper as well. Currently it is unclear if the method's China is using to pull its economy out of a rut will be successful or if Italy will continue to question the EU's spending plans.

Technology stocks have their own challenges: The fate of the market is also dependent on the habits of investors who may or may not yet be ready to get back in bed with the technology companies who did them wrong at the end of 2018. Last year was certainly a mixed bag for technology stock with Amazon, Netflix, Apple and Facebook all pushing various stock benchmarks to new heights before each experiencing serious losses before the end of the year. Part of this was reminiscent of the dotcom boom as certain stocks were simply deemed to be too expensive when compared to the company as a whole. Essentially, investors started off optimistic only to become afraid that earnings wouldn't meet their previous optimistic expectations.

This is not even taking into account that many of these companies are facing problems with operations that will take time to resolve. For example, Apple is currently having problems in China where it is facing increased competition from local alternatives to the iPhone and manufacturing concerns with a key production hub.

Success will need to be multifaceted: All told, it is clear that the economy needs to grow at a steady pace in the coming months if it hopes to deliver the types of corporate earnings that investors are looking for. However, if the economy grows too quickly then investors may end up having to worry about increased interest rates. Likewise, if the Fed can find a middle ground and the trade war winds down, and Europe and China both stabilize then a stock price recovery could be in the cards.

Consider the cycle
Getting to know the difference between the stock market and economic cycles and the manner they relate to the performance of the stock is one of the determining factors for timing strategies and the structure of the portfolio. For one, did you know that the bullish market usually peaks before the peak of the economy? A new bearish approach thus can start even when the economy is growing. By the time the Fed comes out with an announcement concerning a potential recession in the economy, it would be a good time to get aggressive and begin to put more investment into the stocks. You need to learn the reason why the

economy and the stocks tend to peak at different times and the way you can structure a portfolio, so you can maximize the returns. Though it is good to keep in mind, the time in the market as opposed to timing the market would be the best investment approach.

Defining and differentiating the market and the economy: Investors at the present include people such as asset managers, pension funds, banks, and insurance firms and they are the ones that collectively affect what is the market. The market is a reference to the capital markets that happens to be a marketplace for the investing parties to buy and sell securities like stocks, mutual funds, and particular bonds. When you hear concerning the economy, it is a reference to the consumers, financial institutions, firms, and the governing bodies of the economy then mean a financial setting or environment.

Understanding the difference between the economic and the market cycles, the manner they relate to the performance of the investment can assist when it comes to determining the optimal strategies and portfolio structures. For one, the bull market for the stocks usually reaches a peak and begins declining before the peak of the economy. As such, a new bearish approach for stocks may start even as the economy grows even if it is at a slow pace.

Choosing the best sector according to business cycles: In the big picture perspective, the place where the stock market and economy tend to overlap would be in business. This is there for different reasons, but it is mainly because of the fact that businesses drive the economic system and are why there is a stock market in the first place. It is this reason why the investors tend to look at the business cycle and select the industries they would invest according to the historical trends that are going on within the different phases within the particular cycle.

- Early stage: At this time, the economy is in recovery from the recently concluded or concluding recession. Credit is beginning to increase as the monetary policy becomes easier and this adds money and liquidity to the weakened state of the economy. The corporate returns start then to increase considering there is a higher level of aggregate demand. The best sectors would be the service and financial sectors during this phase.

- Mid-cycle stage: This has been termed as the longest phase within the business cycle. The economy may be doing well, though the growth appears to be moderating. The interest rates seem to be at the low points, which attract people to continue borrowing and spending money. The corporate returns are also at the very peak during this time as the aggregate demand is also at the very peak. The best sectors for investment at this time would be the industrial sector, as well as basic materials and the IT sector.

- Late stages: The level of economic growth starts to go into a plateau kind of formation and appears to overheat as the level of inflation climbs higher and the stocks are expensive as compared to the level of earnings. The optimal sectors to invest in at this stage would be the energy and utility sector, which are more stable, and value rather than growth oriented.

- Recession phase: The economic activity and corporate profits would be experiencing a decline at this time and the interest rates are on their way up as the Fed works toward fighting off the inflation. The optimal sectors for investment at this time would be the same ones that ought to be utilized during the late phase which is the energy and utility sectors because they tend to show the most stability.

Current point in the cycle: With the news recently concerning the rate hike, everyone should be asking themselves about where the country is in the market cycle in order to adequately prepare and find the right trades, which could set up in the future. There is one thing, which is for sure, and it is that no one is in a perpetually easing environment. The Federal Reserve claimed they were expecting at least two more increases within the rate this present year and they gave a hint that there would be a potential fourth depending on the level of the economic activity.

The typical market cycle may be identified through consideration of two components within the economy and these would be the bonds as well as the commodity pricing. At the time the commodities increase and the bonds decline, the market cycle would then be seen as experiencing the middle to late stages of expansion and the traders need to be playing any bullish price moves as the late stage opportunities within the bullish trend. When the commodities fall, and the bonds go up, the market cycle is then seen as the middle to late stage contraction and the traders ought to be playing early bottom picking trades and late stage bearish trend trades.

When the global commodity price valuations are considered, it is possible to see that the commodities have become low and this may result in an increase in the level of the commodities in the future, which is a part of the signs related to late stage in the market cycle. The expansion concerning global commodity prices was lower during the latter parts of 2014 as the oil fell to the recent lows and as the central banks eased from the quantitative easing and revenue creation. Recently before the elections two years ago, the global commodity price went to the lowest level since 2004 and began to climb higher.

Challenges when it comes to market timing: Even though the relations between the stock market and the economy would be made simpler within a particular essay, the market timing can be quite complex and so foolish for the investors to try. There is no magical bell, which can be rung when it is time to get in or out of the stocks. For many of the investing parties, the strategy of buying and holding is effective, and this is especially when it is combined with dollar cost averaging. If one wants to utilize the right elements for buy and hold along with market timing, then it may be worth considering tactical asset allocation, which would allow for better results if they were applied in the right manner. In summary, every manner of investing incorporates a particular degree of market timing. The adequate approach for most investors that want to maximize on returns and reduce on risk would be building the best portfolio for mutual funds of their risk tolerance and objectives.

What history can tell us: Since the inception of the financial times stock exchange, there have been a number of bear markets, which describe markets that have declined significantly from their previous high. Historians go over this past information with the hopes that an analysis of how shares behaved in previous market declines would show what could happen at the present. The reasons for each of the previous 11 Bearish movements within the market are different, though some commentators do claim there are a few key ingredients to these issues. These may indicate if the already battered markets would enter a large crisis and go much further or actually recover. Analysis from Stevenson from Fidelity Personal implied the sell-offs were linked with an economic recession or an overvaluation of the stocks.

The sentiments were shared by JP Morgan, who had overseen the most extreme of the bearish movements within the economy, since the great depression. Though, Morgan claimed there were additional ingredients to the matter and these were extreme movements within the price of commodities like oil and an aggressive increase in the rate of interest rates by Federal Reserve. JP Morgan claimed that the research it had done on the matter showed the bearish approaches in the market required a recession or an overvaluation.
Apparently, when one of these or even both is apparent, then the market falls would not end at 20 percent below the previous high, but they would go on declining.

A good example, in this case, would be the tech bubble and the global financial crisis, though, in both of these cases, the overvaluation of the stocks was the thing to blame and not so much on the recession of the economy. In fact, they were the factors that caused the recessions in both cases. During the tech bubble, everyone was suddenly interested in the theme of internet-based firms and the promising value they could create which led to an overvaluation of every internet platform even if they were not necessarily worth that much. People not acquainted with the tech sector carried out a lot of the investing. They wanted to be part of the wave of investing that would supposedly carry on indefinitely. As soon as investors started to realize the market was reversing and the stocks were not worth what had been put down, everyone started a sell-off. This led to the small recession that can be noted during the start of the 21st century. The same is true with the housing boom, which attracted loans for the housing sector. As soon as the reversal began, the interest rates hiked, and people were caught off guard leading to foreclosures and mass evictions.

Chapter 2: Investing in Value Vs. Investing in Growth

Value investing

Value investing is one of the most effective and well-known means of picking stocks and has been ever since it was developed by a pair of professors out of Colombia University in the 1930s. While it is quite easy to understand, be prepared to put in some practice before you can use it easily on the open market. To start, all you will need to do is to find a company that is currently worth more than what its current stock price indicates.

When you find a company whose value compared to its fundamentals is where you want it to be, you are going to want to jump in as quickly as possible as the market is bound to correct itself sooner than later which means if you wait even a minute too long then you are going to find yourself having a difficult time making a profit

When it comes to value investing, the most important thing to keep in mind is that there is a difference between stocks that are currently undervalued for one reason or another and those stocks that are actually almost worthless. Fail to make the right distinction and you will end up buying into stocks that are only going to decrease in value. an example, if a company's stock was previously trading at about $25 per share and it suddenly drops to $10, this doesn't mean that you will automatically want to put it in the buy camp until you determine what caused the drop. This is because the drop could be a perfectly appropriate response by the market to an overall decrease in the company's value. To ensure the stock is the bargain it appears to be you would need to take a closer look at the fundamentals.

Legendary money maker Warren Buffet is perhaps the most successful proponent of this strategy of all time. In 1967 shares of Berkshire Hathaway were worth only $12 per share and he held them until 2002 when they were worth a staggering $70,900 per share. Now, these results are certainly the exception, not the rule, but they go to show just how powerful this form of investing can be if it is done correctly.

In order to grasp the effectiveness of value investing there are a few things you need to understand.

Every company has an intrinsic value: All of value investing can be summed up with an idea that most people

18

learned at a very young age, you can save a substantial amount of money if you wait to buy things when they are on sale. While everyone understands that if you buy a television on sale you are getting the same bang for your buck as if you buy it at full price, most fail to see the fact that the same general principle applies to the stock market just as much as it does to consumer products. The only difference is that with the stock market it is the stock whose price is changing while the intrinsic value of the company remains the same.

Value investing creates a margin of safety: The margin of safety that is created when you buy stocks at value prices exists because you naturally have less to lose if the stock doesn't perform in the way you would like. This is one of the keys to value investing's effectiveness as they are naturally a significantly safer option that investing in speculative stocks which are likely to drop in price at the drop of a hat.

Value investors seek out stocks that they believe to currently be undervalued under the assumption that the price will eventually normalize as the market is bound to self-correct eventually. With this reasoning, the lowered price isn't the risk it is normally perceived as because the value investor has reason to believe that the price is currently experiencing little more than a slight downturn. For example, if you purchase a stock you believe to be undervalued at $66 and then watch it increase to what you believe to be the accurate valuation of $100 then you made $34 per share by simply waiting for the market to correct its error.

Furthermore, if the price continues moving in a positive direction to the tune of an additional $10 then you would have made a total of $44 per share as opposed to the $10 per share profit you likely would have made if you had held off buying until the price had completely stabilized.

Know the numbers: As a general rule, you are going to want to use this investment strategy to purchase stocks that have a value that is at least 30 percent greater than its current price. With this safety net available you should be free to generate the maximum amount of returns while still minimizing the potential for overall risk.

Additionally, you are going to want to look for companies who have a price to earnings (P/E) ratio in the bottom 10 percent of all equity securities. The price/earnings to growth ratio, which is the P/E ratio divided by the growth rate of the company's earnings, should be less than one.

The P/E ratio will allow you to determine the share price when compared to the earnings per share, starting with the current value of a share of the stock you are interested in. You will want to take this number and divide it by the last round of reported earnings that the company experienced. For example, if a company had a current share price of $43 as well as $1.95 worth of earnings per share then to find the P/E ratio you would simply divide 43 by 1.95 to get a P/E ratio of 22.05.

The price to earnings ratio can also be thought of as the amount you would need to invest in a company in order to see a $1 return in the form of earnings from the company. In the preceding example, investors appear to currently be willing to pay just over $22 in order to see $1 of company profit. As a general rule of thumb, the higher the P/E ratio is, the greater the overall level of performance that investors expect from the stock in question.

If you find yourself dealing with a company with a low P/E ratio then it is possible that the company is currently undervalued, especially if it has been seeing record profits recently that may not yet have had time to make it into a quarterly report. While negative P/E ratios can be calculated, companies that are not currently posting a positive profit number list their P/E ratio as N/A.

The P/E ratio is not without some limits, however, which are important to keep in mind in order to use them correctly. First and foremost, the industry of the company you are interested in needs to be taken into account as the results will vary dramatically. Additionally, this means that you cannot directly compare the P/E ratio of various companies, assuming they are not in the same industry as well. Furthermore, the P/E ratio will not take into account the potential for risk and reward that taking on additional debt can sometimes afford. Finally, it is important to keep in mind that many publicly traded companies use complicated accounting techniques to obfuscate the true results of their most recent quarter which can lead to false results as well.

Furthermore, the stock price should never be more than the tangible book value and the company should have less debt than it does equity. The company's current assets should be at least twice that of its current liabilities and its dividend yield should be a minimum of two-thirds of its long-term bond yield. Its earnings growth should be a minimum of 7 percent per annum when compounded for the last 10 years.

Finally, it is important to always factor in a margin of safety as well. A margin of safety is simply a little wiggle room when it comes to potential errors that may have occurred when you were calculating the intrinsic value of the company. To add in a margin of error, all you need to do is subtract 10 percent from the intrinsic value number you came up with.

Growth investing

While value investors tend to focus on stocks that are currently trading for less than their true value, growth investors tend to focus on the future potential they see in a company, regardless of what shares might be going for in the here and now. Growth investors typically buy stocks in companies that are currently showing signs of trading at a rate that is greater than their true intrinsic value under the assumption that this is a sign the intrinsic value is on the rise. Ultimately, when everything is said and done, growth investors want to increase their wealth via capital appreciation is either the short or the long-term.

Capital gains are key: Growth investors tend to invest in companies whose earnings are realistically expected to grow at a greater than average rate when compared to the industry average or the market as a whole. As such, the focus tends to be on younger companies as these are the ones that are ultimately going to have the most growth potential. The idea here is that growth in earnings/revenues will ultimately result in higher stock prices in the future. Growth investors tend to stay on the lookout for investments in industries that are rapidly expanding and where new technologies and services are currently in development. This results in an overall focus on capital gains as opposed to dividends as these companies are going to be reinvesting all of their earnings in growth.

Key facts to watch for: There is no perfect formula when it comes to evaluating the potential of a given company which means it is always going to require a certain amount of personal judgement and interpretation. Growth investors do have a variety of criteria and guidelines by which to create a framework to separate likely companies from bad actors, but these all need to be used with the specifics of a given company in mind. Above all else, it is important that you always consider the particular of the given company's situation, as well as its current relationship with its past performance in the context of industry standards. As such, it is common for specific criterion or guidelines to be more or less relevant across different companies and industries.

Viable growth stocks can be found across virtually all sectors and exchanges, though they will always appear in higher concentrations in industries that are currently experiencing high degrees of growth. General guidelines in this area include the following:

Strong historical earnings growth: As a general rule, the companies that you are considering investing in need to show strong earnings growth for anywhere between the last five and 10 years. What indicates strong growth varies based on the size of the company. If the company, you are considering is worth more than four billion dollars then you will want to see at least five percent growth. If the company, you are considering is worth more than 400 million dollars and less than four billion dollars then you will want to see at least seven percent growth. For companies smaller than that you will want to see a minimum of 12 percent growth per year. The basic idea is that if the company has displayed good growth in the recent past, it's likely to continue doing so moving forward.

Strong potential for future growth: The earnings announcement for a company either happens quarterly or once per year. These announcements are always made on specific dates during the earnings season and are proceeded by estimates. It is these estimates that you will want to focus on as they will determine which companies are beating average rates. It is important to then see if the company meets or exceeds expectations as this will have a huge impact on its standings in the coming months.

Large profit margins: To determine the pretax profit margin of a given company you start by taking its total profit and subtracting out all of the expenses and then dividing by the total number of sales. This is a very important metric to consider as a company can have very high levels of growth while still having poor earnings which indicates that something serious is going on at some point in the process which means you are going to want to stay away no matter what. Generally speaking, if a company exceeds its profit margins for the past five years, while also exceeding industry standards, then you can assume you are on the right track.

Strong return on equity: The return on equity a company boasts is a measure of its overall profitability as it reveals how much profit a company generates with the money that investors have put up thus far. It can be calculated by starting with the net income and then dividing it by overall shareholder equity. You will typically want to compare the current ROE of a company with its previous five-year average as well as the previous five year average of the industry as a whole. If the ROE is either stable or increasing, then you can assume management is ensuring that returns are being generated from any investments.

Strong stock performance: In general, if a stock cannot realistically double in five years, it's probably not a growth stock. Keep in mind, a stock's price would double in seven years with a growth rate of just 10 percent. To double in five years, the growth rate must be 15 percent which is almost certainly something that's feasible for young companies in rapidly expanding industries.

GARP Investing
Growth at a reasonable price (GARP) investing is a mixture between value investing and growth investing. To take advantage of this type of investing you are going to want to be on the lookout for companies that are somewhat undervalued at the moment that, nevertheless, have the potential for sustainable growth in the future. Ideally, you will want to look for stocks that are less undervalued than with value investing with somewhat less impressive future potential than if you were following the growth investing plan.

GARP investing is primarily concerned with the growth of the prospective company which means that with this method you will always want to be on the lookout for companies with positive earnings for the past five years along with positive earnings projections for the next five years as well. Unlike pure growth investing, the ideal range of growth for these companies is going to be between 25 and 50 percent. The idea here is that the somewhat lower growth rate results in a lower overall amount of risk which equates to greater profits overall.

GARP investing also shares many of the metrics for potential companies with growth investing, though the levels you will need to look for are going to be lower overall. A good GARP company is one that sees positive earnings momentum along with positive cash flow. Besides that, you are going to have more freedom overall when it comes to choosing the best companies as subjectivity is an inherent part of GARP investing.

Additionally, you are going to want to remain of the lookout for P/E ratios that exceed those which are looked for when it comes to value investing while also making sure they are lower than those used with growth investing. While a growth investor needs a P/E ratio that is at least 50 times greater than earnings, GARP investors are going to be looking in the 15 to 25 range.

Chapter 3: Cloud Pattern Trading

The Ichimoku cloud pattern is a type of investing and charting system that is purpose-built to be useable in virtually every market. It has several unique characteristics, but its primary strength lies in the fact that it utilizes multiple different points of data as a means of giving the person using it a comprehensive view of the current price action. This more insightful view, coupled with the fact that it is a very visual system in general, makes it easy for traders to quickly separate potential trades with a low probability of success from those that are more likely to work out in the end.

The Ichimoku cloud pattern was developed by a newspaper reporter by the name of Goichi Hosada who began developing his system before the start of World War II. He worked on it for nearly 30 years before releasing it to the public in 1968 in a book that revealed the final version of the system. It has been extensively used by Asian traders ever since, though it did not make its way west until the early 90s where it was relegated to the sidelines by most due to its apparent complexity. It is only in the last decade that Western traders have wised up and started taking advantage of its usefulness.

When translated, its name means equilibrium chart at a glance, which not only describes the system accurately but also outlines how it is used. The Ichimoku cloud pattern uses five separate components or lines, not individually, but rather all together to make it as easy to see the big picture when it comes to price action as possible. As such, a quick glance at the Ichimoku chart should be enough to provide you with everything you need to know when it comes to the strength and momentum of a given trend as well as the sentiment behind it.

Price action is typically gauged based on the perspective of whether it is in equilibrium or not with the market as a whole. The Ichimoku chart works on the assumption that the market is a direct reflection of human behavior which moves through its own states of equilibrium. Each of its 5 components then provides their own reflection of this equilibrium.

What follows is a brief overview of the five different equilibrium lines and how they are calculated. Additional detail is provided below.

Tenkan Sen: This is known as the turning line and it is found by looking at the previous nine periods and adding together the highest high and the lowest low before dividing by 2 for each period.

Chikou Span: This is known as the lagging line and it is found by taking the price at closing of the current period and shifting it backwards 26 periods.

Kijun Sen: This is known as the standard line and it is found by looking at the previous nine periods and adding together the highest high and the lowest low before dividing by 2 for each period.

Senkou Span A: This is known as the initial leading line and it can be found by adding together the kijun sen and the tenkan sen before dividing by 2 and then finally shifting the resulting amount forward 26 periods.

Senkou Span B: This is known as the second leading line and it is found by looking at the previous 52 periods and adding together the highest high and the lowest low before dividing by 2 for each period and then shifting the result forward 26 periods.

Settings

When it comes to the Ichimoku chart, each line has either one or two different settings based on the number of periods you are looking at in the moment. The number 26 is pulled from the number of days in the standard Japanese business month, 9 comes from the number of days in a week and a half (minus Sunday) and 52 represents two months. While these numbers obviously don't line up with the cryptocurrency trading timeframe, they are still effective and thus should not be changed.

Tenkan sen: When the tenkan sen is similar to the 9-period simple moving average at first blush, it is actually a very different beast entirely as it actually measures the lowest low and highest high of the average price for the previous nine periods. Using the average of pricing extremes over this period of time make it possible to provide a better overall measure of equilibrium as opposed to using the average of the closing price for the same period of time.

The tenkan sen is known to frequently see periods of time where it flattens out, while the more traditional simple moving average does not. This is due to the fact that the tenkan sen makes use of a pair of averages rather than just the one. What this means is that if the price is ranging then the tenkan sen can be counted on to clearly show the midpoint of the given range due to its flatness. If it is flat, it is essentially indicating that the last 9 periods lack any type of strong trend.

Generally speaking, this then leads to a more accurate prediction of the price support level most of the time. This is decidedly not the case if the price remains higher than the tenkan sen while at the same time breaking lower than the current standard moving action several times in a row. This is due to the fact that the tenkan sen tends to be more conservative in its overall calculations which means it reacts less to smaller price movements in most instances. Furthermore, if the chart ends up being bearish then the tenkan sen will take on the role of resistance level.

It is also important to keep in mind that the angle the tenkan sen demonstrates is also useful when it comes to providing you with an idea of the relative momentum of individual price movements over the 9-period span. If the angle is quite steep, then it indicates that the price rose in an almost vertical ascent over a very short period of time which means it is currently riding on a lot of momentum. If the rise is more languid, then it means the price is still rising but it is doing so while only gaining minimal momentum.

The kijun sen and the tenkan sen both measure shorter trends. Of the two, the tenkan sen is faster due to the fact that it looks at 9 periods rather than 26. Unfortunately, this also makes it less reliable when it comes to determining an accurate trend in the moment when compared to the other components of the Ichimoku chart. Nevertheless, if the price breaches the tenkan sen line then this should be thought of as a strong indicator that change

30

is coming, though you will still want to independently confirm it before pulling the trigger on any lingering trades.

Kijun sen: The kijun sen line is one of the most useful lines of them all because it can be used to fill a wide variety of different roles. First and foremost, it is an excellent measure of the individual ups and downs a given stock might experience over a longer overall timeframe than the tenkan sen which naturally makes it the more reliable of the two as well. The kijun sen is especially useful if the price appears to be ranging as it can be used to determine the vertical midpoint of the current range.

Once the price has moved past the first of the kijun prices in the given timeframe, you can quickly expect the kijun sen to start moving in the direction of the new trend. This is useful as it makes it possible to measure shorter trends overall as you can then measure then by noting the direction the kijun sen is currently moving or by instead considering its angle in relation to the overall level of strength and momentum of the related trend. Due to its longer timeframe, it also works as an excellent means of either resistance or support.

A majority of the time you can expect the price to fixate on the kijun sen in a repeatable fashion, moving back and forth around it as the kijun sen tends to be very receptive to equilibrium movement. This means that if the momentum reaches either end of the spectrum the price will almost always quickly follow along. This ultimately leads to a rubber band effect that is typically visible when the price returns to the realm of the kijun sen as it will likely continue to double back on itself until it regains its equilibrium. Finally, the kijun sen frequently makes an effective stop loss or entry point as it is almost never going to equate to a point that is high risk.

Chikou span: The chikou span line is the rarest of all of the lines to see in action on a chart which makes it one of the most interesting as well. This is the case as you will rarely be able to pick out a point where the lines shift singularly in a specific direction as a means of gaining additional detail about the current state of the market. To do so you will need to find the close price and then shift it backwards 26 periods in order to find the pattern for the trend over the previous weeks.

If this exercise ends up proving the current price point is the lowest the price has been for the past month then you can safely assume that further movement is going to be forthcoming and that it will be bearish baring any unexpected developments.

Beyond simply illuminating a given trend, the chikou span is extremely important when it comes to finding the specific levels of resistance and support when compared to other recent closing prices. This can be done by simply adding a horizontal line to the existing chikou points to determine what the current levels are as well as the best ways to take advantage of them moving forward.

Senkou span A: The senkou spans together are responsible for the cloud from which Ichimoku derives its name. This is another time-shifted line except that this line is time-shifted forward. It showcases the traditional span of the kijun sen as well as the tenkan sen which ultimately makes it possible to determine the equilibrium quite easily.

Generally speaking, it also makes it possible for users to easily find the future price action when it is compared to what is currently going on in the space.

Senkou span B: Span B has the greatest amount of equilibrium of all the various Ichimoku lines thanks to the fact that it takes into account both the highs and lows of all 52 periods. With that done, you will then want to take those measurements and shift them forward an additional 26 periods in order to determine what is likely to happen in the next month. From this point, you should then be able to more easily determine the equilibrium based on the amount of potential price action that is likely to occur which should make it easier than it might otherwise be to make a properly informed decision in the moment. While you can still be successful using only senkou spans, doing so tends to limit the effectiveness of the Ichimoku cloud as a whole and thus is not recommended.

Final thoughts
As a general rule, you should keep in mind that the overall thickness of the cloud can have a few different meanings. In fact, the depth of the cloud serves to indicate the current level of volatility you can expect from the stock in question with a thicker cloud indicating that volatility is at historic levels. In order to trade successfully with these types of signals, you will need to remember that a thick cloud indicates a greater amount of resistance or support depending on external variables. Keeping this fact in mind will thus make it easier for you to ensure your trading strategy is right for you.

Generally speaking, clouds tend to have either flat bottoms or flat tops, both of which serve to indicate their role when it comes to the overall equilibrium. If a flat kijun sen creates a rubber band effect, then a flat span B will do the same as it represents the midpoint of a specific price in a given trend based on that month's data. Based on the fact that the price is always going to lean towards its equilibrium, the flatter span B can thus be thought of as a strong expression of this type of equilibrium to the point that it actually becomes an attractor of the price.

However, if the trend ends up being bullish, then you can likely expect span B to generate a larger cloud that includes a flat bottom along with a bearish trend that should appear as a flat top. If such a thing does come to pass you will want to ensure you remain cautious when it comes to trades that exit or enter the cloud.

As an example, if you find yourself exiting a bullish cloud that includes a flat bottom, instead of placing your entry order at 10 pips beneath the senkou span B you would want to go even lower as a way of avoiding the pull of span B which should also help to minimize the overall number of false breakouts that you have to suffer through as a result.

Chapter 4: Price Action Trading

While many traders make use of complicated indicators that have to do with reading charts and drawing figures based on complex formulas, as a someone who is relatively new to the idea of actively trading you are likely going to be much better served by starting with price action trading instead. While some traders may turn their noses up at anything that professional traders aren't currently using, the reality is that indicator-based trading only works for the experts because they have already learned how to compensate for its flaws. As such, if you are brand new to the process then you are going to want to start with something that can be understood easily and work on improving your trade percentage before you need to start worrying about finding more complicated ways to pick the stocks that you ultimately do trade.

At its most basic, price action can be thought of as a way for a trader to determine the current state of the market based on the way that prices are currently acting as opposed to what one of dozens of different indicators has to say about it after the fact. As such, if you are a trader that is interested in getting started as quickly as possible then sticking with price action trading, for now, can save you serious time as you only have to spend your time and focus studying the market as it is in the present. Additionally, focusing exclusively on the price and the price alone will help you to avoid much of the unnecessary information that is constantly circling the market, blocking out the static and increasing your overall chance of success.

Starting strong: In order to determine when to trade using price action, you are going to need to use the trading platform that came with the brokerage you chose and utilize what are known as price bars. Price bars are a representation of price information over a specific period of time broken down into weekly, daily, 1 hour, 30-minute or 5-minute intervals. In order to create an accurate price bar, you need the open price for the given stock in the chosen time period, the high for the time period, the low for the time period and the closing price. With this data, you should end up with a box with a line through it (also known as a candle). The line represents the high and the low for the day while the edges of the box show the opening and closing prices.

In addition to summarizing the information for the time frame in question, it also provides relevant information for your purposes. This includes the range of the stock which is a representation of how volatile the market currently is. The bigger the box in relation to the line, the more active the market currently is and the more volatile as well. The more volatile the market currently is, the more risk you undertake when making a specific move.

In addition to the range, you are going to want to consider the physical orientation of the box, if the close price is above the open price, then the market improved over the time frame and if the close is below the open then the market lost value. You are also going to want to take into account the size of the box as a whole. The bigger the box, the stronger the market is overall.

What this type of strategy provides you with is a clear idea of what the levels of resistance and support are like for the time period in question. This, in turn, allows you to pick trades with a higher degree of certainty. All you need to do is keep in mind that if demand is stronger than supply then the price is going to increase, and vice versa.

Secondary price bar: If you add an additional price bar to your existing analysis then you will find that you have created a pair of cornerstones that will make it easier for you to test the price while ensuring it has the proper context as well. Essentially, the second bar is going to provide a way to determine if the data from the first bar is actually relevant or merely an irrelevant outlier. Specifically, it is useful when it comes to things like determining if a bar that appears wide is actually just on par with the other bars from the same timeframe.

This, in turn, makes it possible for you to describe the price action in a more precise way than would otherwise be possible. What's more, having a second price bar will allow you to determine if the price level will then be enough to either break through the existing levels of resistance or support. If the second bar shows the same level of support or resistance, then it is unlikely the price action will remain strong enough in order to break through it. Furthermore, if the two candles both have differing levels of resistance or support it is far more likely that a quality breakthrough will be made.

Third price bar: Once you add in a third price bar you will be able to confirm your existing hypothesis that adding in the second bar allowed you to create. This third bar should then be shown to much in such a way that it either completely confirms or denies the expectations the market presented you with to that point. The idea here is that if a market is already strong then it will continue to be so, and if it is weak then it will continue to be weak. If the market lacks inertia, then it is possible for a change to materialize at virtually any time. It is thus important to ensure you keep in mind that even with three bars the results are still only going to apply to the short-term and taking this pattern to be anything other than short-term is going to be a huge risk assuming you don't follow up properly.

Candlestick patterns: One of the most common types of candlestick patterns is what is known as the long black line or simply the long black wick. When charting a candlestick pattern if you see the long black wick then you should know that it indicates that the market is in a period of bearishness. This means that during the trading period that is being charted, the currency or currency pairs that you are charting moved both up and down in a wide range throughout the period being charted. Additionally, it can indicate that the price started near the high point for the day and ended at a point much lower closer to the end of the day.

Alternatively, a long white wick indicates a period where the market was bullish which means that the exact opposite, when compared with the long black wick, is true. This ultimately means that while the price of the currency or currencies in question moved through several whipsaw periods, the end result worked out to be that the start of the period saw lower prices while the end of the trading period was privy to higher prices overall.

This type of activity can also manifest itself via what is known as a spinning top. A spinning top has a small wick even though the price of the currency or currencies in question moved repeatedly throughout a given time period, thought the overall amount of movement was relatively minor. This type of wick can be either white or black and if it appears it is often taken to mean that the market is unsure as a whole about the currency or currency pair and its future.

Furthermore, a doji candlestick wick can look like either a plus sign, an inverted cross or a regular cross depending on the mood of the market. Without additional context, a doji wick is going to be neutral and it typically forms when the amount that the currency or currency pair started at is essentially the same as when it closes. It can often be taken as a sign that a reversal pattern is going to soon come into play.

Candlestick strategies
3-bar reversal pattern: First and foremost, you are only going to want to target stocks that are strongly trending in one direction. Second, the low (downtrend) or high (uptrend) bar needs to occur in the middle of a candlestick. Finally, the final bar needs to close either above the high of the first two candlesticks. With this standard in place, it will then be painfully obvious once a given trend has reversed.

This strategy works in a variety of timeframes. As an example, assume you are working off of the 5-minute chart before detecting a stock that hit its low and then sharply reversed upwards. The third bar in the series would then close at a point that is higher than the highs of both of the other bars. While you can move forward if the close is above the high of the middle candlestick, it is better to know what the third candle is doing for added insurance.

The exit strategy for this pattern is just a simple moving average or even a price target. Just be sure you watch it closely and you should be fine. A good rule of thumb with this pattern is a 3 to 1 risk and reward ratio for the trade. Additionally, it is important to keep in mind that this strategy can generate quick returns no matter what time of day it is and in any market type.

These days, more and more day traders are trying to fake one another out when it comes to specific trades. Unfortunately, the 3-bar reversal pattern is not immune to this problem. One of the main reasons that the 3-bar reversal pattern fails is when volatility isn't high enough. If the market is exceedingly choppy, then the formation you are looking for is really going to be nothing more than a pause in the overall action.

This means it will not ultimately result in the type upswing or downswing that you are looking for. Adding in additional methods of confirmation before you choose your entry point will make it easier to avoid these false signals.

Hook reversal: The hook reversal pattern is most frequently found in charts with shorter timeframes. They can appear during any type of trend and are especially useful when it comes to learning about a new trend that will mark a reversal for the current status quo. This type of pattern is known to appear with a higher low as well as a lower high when compared to the candles of the previous day. You can tell this pattern from the rest because the size difference between the body of the first and second bar is quite small when compared to other, similar patterns.

If this type of forms around a trend that is positive, then the open will naturally be nearer the previous high while the low will form near the previous low. This pattern is frequently associated with other more frequently seen positions as the body of the second candle will often form with the first candle's body. The strength you can attribute to this signal will often be tied directly to the overall strength of the trend with a stronger trend naturally having a stronger signal to give off.

Outside reversal: This is a price chart pattern that can be seen when the high and low for a given day both exceed the high of the previous session's trading day. This pattern is known as an engulfing bearish pattern, assuming the second bar shows a downtrend, and an engulfing bullish pattern if the second bar is a positive pattern. This pattern is especially useful if you are looking for a means of identifying price movement for the near future in addition to getting a sneak peek at what the related trend will be. It typically occurs at the point where the first price bar drops outside the range of the previous price bar when its high is above the previous high and the low is as well. As a general rule, if the outside reversal occurs at the level of resistance then the signal is bearish and if it occurs at the support level then it is bullish.

Chapter 5: Consider Dividend Stocks

Simply stated, dividend investing is the type of investing that allows you the chance to pull out big sums of money from the investments that you make. The dividends are the results of high-yield trades, and they will pay you on a regular basis to be able to make the money that you need when you are doing various types of investing in different things.

The biggest benefit of dividend investing is that people who invest in dividends from a company are able to get the most out of it. They are able to receive regular payments from the company, unlike other types of investing that are not exactly stable. People who participate in dividend investing will receive a return on their investment on a regular basis and by the amount of money that a company makes. In general, this is a rising amount and something that shows the health of a company and how much they are able to make things better for the people who have invested in the company.

When someone does dividend investing, they usually do it with a company that is going to remain stable over the next few years. The companies that allow dividend investing are already established, and they want to make sure that the people who invest in the company are able to get the amount of money that they want. For that reason, they are always working to make sure that their stocks are rising and that the company is as valuable as the investors would like it to be.

When a company has a large profit, they will normally split it into two parts. This is the dividend aspect of the investment. The company that splits it into two will put half of the amount of the profit back into the business and the other half into the stocks of the business, or the pockets of those investors. It is important to note that when a company does this, they are doing so only to help out their investors and show them that they are actually able to make a profit off of the business.

Dividend yield formula: Not all stock dividends are created equal. Just because a company pays out a dividend, or even has a history of doing so regularly, doesn't mean that its dividends are going to be as strong as they could potentially be. The best way to measure the quality of a company's dividends is through what is known as the dividend yield formula. This formula is a calculation that makes it easy to determine how much a specific company is paying out in comparison to its overall stock price.

Essentially, the equation involves taking the amount of dividend that a stock pays out yearly, dividing that amount by the price each share is currently worth and then multiplying the result by 100. The equation looks like this:

Dividend yield = annual dividend / current share price x 100

For example, assume that a company pays out 40 cents per share each quarter for a total of $1.60 per share per year. If its stock price is $30 a share, then is dividend yield would be just over five percent ($1.50/$30 x 100).

When it comes to determining the amount of dividend that a given stock is paying out, it is important to keep in mind that bigger numbers aren't always better, especially if the price of one of the stocks in question is also bigger as well. This is what makes the dividend yield formula so useful as it makes it easy to measure just how much cash flow is being generated by every dollar that is being invested in a given stock.

As an example, assume that one company has a share price of $100 and pays out a total dividend of $2 per year while a second company pays out just a dollar per year in total, but its share price is just $25. The second company is actually a much better deal because it generates a dividend of four percent while the first company generates a dividend return of just two percent. This means investing in the second company would result in twice as much overall profit in the long-term.

Picking the right companies: It is a good idea to make sure that you are picking everything in the right way so that, when the time comes, you can truly cash in on the dividends. Choosing the right ones will allow you to do so more quickly and will give you the chance to make even more money.

- Profits: The profits of the company are the number one thing that you should look at when you are deciding whether or not to choose them for your dividend investment. A company needs to have high profits for you to choose them and they need to show that they are going to have these profits for a long time in the future. It is a great way to make sure that the profits are going the right direction and to make sure that you are going to be able to make money off of the investment that you make.

- Size of Payouts: You can always check the size of the payouts that the company has made in the past to find out what type of payments you can expect from the company. By simply looking at the trading profile of the company, you will be able to see how much they pay out, how often and what that takes out of the profits that they have made.

  When you look at this amount, you need to consider all of the aspects of the payouts. This also includes the initial investment amount. Compare that amount to what you are planning on investing in the company and see if the payouts will be worth it for what you are going to invest in the company. It is important to make sure that you are looking at all of this information in a way as if you were going to actually invest in the company.

- Company history: In investing, it is not uncommon for history to repeat itself so if a company had issues in the past, there is a high chance that they will have issues in the future. Keep this in mind when you are investing in the company and even when you are just researching the options that you have when it comes to investing in the company. By looking at the history portfolio of the company, you will be able to make sure that you are getting the most out of the experience and that you are going to see what is going on with the company so that you can make more important decisions about the future.

Buy and hold strategy

The buy and hold strategy are probably the easiest strategy that you can use, but it is also very effective. As the name implies, the buy and hold strategy is about buying a particular asset and holding on to it as its price increases. You can then sell it at a profit. Although this strategy may seem very simple, many investors have gained millions of profits using this basic strategy. When it comes to following the buy low, sell high principle, then the buy and hold strategy is the way to go.

It is important to note that you should not use this strategy blindly. Before you buy something and investing in it, you should first study it and determine if its price would most likely increase or decrease in the future. If after careful consideration of the circumstances, it appears that the price of a particular asset will most likely increase, then that is the time for you to make an investment. However, if it is the contrary, then feel free to do more research and look for a better investment.

The key factor to look for is value. Look for something that has good value but is currently priced lower than it deserves. If you buy that particular asset today, then its price will most likely increase in the future. You can then sell it at profit.

If you are interested in practicing this type of trading, then the best course of action is to limit yourself to a single field and then learn everything you can about the state of the field today.

Once the investment has been made, it mostly becomes a waiting game. As previously noted, a majority of the companies that you invest in will ultimately end in a loss, some will maintain a stagnant growth rate and the remaining few will generate a profit. Depending on the rate of returns you are seeing you can then use some of these profits to reinvest in a large share of the growing company or redistribute them into other businesses depending on your goals and time frame.

Assuming you have time to wait, this strategy has a number of benefits, the biggest of these is what is known as compounding, which is the idea that it is important to reinvest as much of your early profits as possible back into the initial investment as a means of maximizing your long-term results. Reinvesting both early and regularly is crucial to maximizing your profits in the long-term and the longer you have to let the profits build upon themselves the more powerful the force of compounding will be.

To understand the true potential of compounding, consider a college student with a fresh master's degree in hand and 40 years to go until retirement. If they want to be a millionaire by the time, they retire all they need to do is to save $900 per month and ensure that their investments generate an average 5 percent return on investment each year. However, if that same person waited 10 years to get started, they would need to save $2,000 per month to hit the same goal. Meanwhile, if they waited 20 years then they would need to save more than $4,000 a month to be at the same place when retirement came knocking.

Aside from getting started as quickly as possible, it is important to understand your personal investment habits in order to ensure that your personal habits are helping, rather than hindering your investments. No strategy is going to be right for everyone and in order to start cutting some from the stack the first thing you will need to do is to consider how long you have until you are going to want to use the funds you have available and how frequently you want to interact with them.

It will also be important to consider your goals when it comes to investing as these can easily affect the ultimate strategy that you choose to pursue. This could be something safe, such as keeping your initial investment intact no matter what, or it could be something with a greater amount of risk and potential reward. The specifics themselves don't matter, what matters is that you take the time to clearly identify your plan and then stick with it once it has been instigated.

Give it time: Once one buys stocks, they tend to want to know the way they are doing in the market performance wise. Though checking up on the stocks on a daily basis is also a bit overkill and is a good way to drive oneself crazy especially if you consider all the ticks of the market that can happen during that time. If your strategy is to hold the investments over the long-term using the buy and hold approach, then it does not make sense to be hung up every day or even on a weekly basis on the pricing difficulties. That is a good way to break your trading ethics and sell or short the stocks even before their appointed time.

That being said, you ought to still check on the investments on a monthly basis in order to see how they are doing. Do not just glance at the portfolio to see the current value. You need to check the individual firms whose stocks you have shares with and look for potential problems or red flag indications. If there are ongoing discussions, for example, that there may be new management coming into the company and this makes you nervous, then you may want to get out of the position as opposed to taking a risk and going ahead.

While purchasing stocks could seem like one of the most daunting prospects, once you get over the first few issues, you are going to find it is much easier than you had believed at first. You need to remember there is no absolute or perfect strategy for buying stocks. A lot of it just settles on educated and targeted guesswork. Though, if you have a willingness to do the research and be patient, then you have a good chance of coming out on top.

Chapter 6: Consider Penny Stocks

The name penny stocks is the general classification given to a wide variety of stocks that can actually trade at anything less than $5.00 per share. In addition to sticking to smaller amounts per share, these types of stocks are going to be able to first be listed after a much less strict overall overview process than they would with the larger exchanges. This means that the company could be completely sound, just untested, or it could be barely more than an idea without even a working business plan, which is where the risk comes in to balance out the potential reward. The potential for reward is great, however, as the low price of penny stocks means that you could easily pick up enough shares to see a significant return from a relatively small amount of positive movement.

While the reward may be great, the specter hanging over all penny stocks is the fact that a majority of them ultimately end up going belly up before they have generated any sort of substantial return for their investors. Despite this fact, the draw of penny stocks is readily apparent when you look at what the estimated return is when compared with that of a similar stock from one of the major markets. As an example, if you have $1,000 to invest and choose to do so in a mundane stock that generates an average rate of return of 10 percent then after 50 years you can expect to make roughly $120,000 for your troubles. In that same period of time, however, if you manage to successfully invest in penny stocks then the total you could make over this same period of time doubles to 20 percent or nearly $10,000,000 total.

Penny stocks offer many advantages over stocks traded on large exchanges. These are advantages that are perfect for a first-time trader, or even an experienced trader that is simply working with an overall smaller investment fund. Penny stocks offer a greater level of volatility, require a smaller investment fund to get started, and are not as susceptible to manipulation from news and financial reports.

Volatility is a lovely thing for a trader. It is the backbone of how a trader makes money. It doesn't matter if a market is bullish or bearish; as long as there is movement in stocks then there is money to be made. It is when stocks are stagnant that profits become elusive. Think about it this way: a fluctuating stock price means that someone is always going to be making money and someone is going to be losing money. A stock that says the same price has no benefit to the trader, as money is simply not changing hands.

The buy-in amount for penny stocks is considerably lower than the starting amount for other types of trading. Investors can get started with as low as one thousand dollars, and a two-thousand-dollar investment fund is more than enough to be adequately positioned for penny stock trading. The starting amounts required for larger exchanges are extreme in comparison and make it so that either you need a large amount of savings to get started, or you are taking huge risks on any single trade.

The low price of penny stocks also means that you can make many more bets than you would in larger markets. An element of positioning that is often overlooked is just how risky a trader feels about any single trade. Traders on larger exchanges that do not have large amounts of capital are less likely to take the risks that they need to make a good profit. With penny stocks this issue is non-existent, and a trader will be able to invest with more confidence knowing that any one trade does not hold as much financial risk.

Market capitalization: Many of the companies in this tier tend to offer goods as opposed to services and they may even be at such an early point that they can still be considered in the startup phase which is why they are equally as likely to fail as they are too succeed, even with the influx of investor capital that being listed on a stock exchange provides. As such, the first step to determining if a penny stock is ultimately going to be worth your time is to consider what is known as market capitalization.

To determine the market capitalization of a given company you simply take the current price of the stock and factor it into the total number of available shares. As an example, if a given company has a share value of $50, as well as 5 million total shares in the market, then you can safely assume that company is worth 250 million dollars.

Companies can also be evaluated based on the expectations that investors have for their future, in addition to, or in spite of, their earnings. Earnings are the total that a company made, typically broken down by quarter, after all their expenses have been paid. Public companies (those traded on the market) are required to report their earnings once every three months in what are also known as earning seasons. These reports are then perused by analysts, so they can get an idea of what the next quarter is likely going to look like. If these estimated results don't end up lining up with previous expectations, then the price of the stock will drop and if it exceeds expectations then it will rise.

Finally, the most complicated variable to get a handle on of all is going to be public opinion. Historically, the stock market is full of examples of companies that experienced extremely high stock prices for a prolonged period of time without actually generating any visible earnings. When investing in rising stocks, public opinion can be worth its weight in gold, but putting it ahead of actual financial statements is always going to be risky as well because public opinion can shift on a dime. Deciding if you are interested in this type of stock will be one of your first periods of direct contact when it comes to risk and reward.

Choose the right type of penny stock: Now it's time for you to start working on personalizing your investment approach and tailoring it to match your specific needs. Penny stocks are not all the same. Yes, they are all lower priced commodities that are much easier to invest in but after that, you'll see a wide range of differences. Most will come under a specific category like biotech, technology, resources, or transportation. Ideally, for a beginner, you should only choose those stocks in areas that you know a little something about. Once you've decided on which industry you want to trade in, get to know the markets, learn the price range of the shares being traded, and any other information that might have an effect on the price.

If you choose an industry you are familiar with then you will be able to better gauge how news events and other factors can have an impact on the price of the stock, you choose to invest in. Remember, knowledge is power, the more you know the lower your level of risk in the investment.

You will need to gather a lot of information in order to make an informed decision. All of the information is out there for the taking but it could require a large investment in time. Some prefer to hire a research service to dig up juicy bits of information to help you in your investment decision. Whatever you choose to do, whether you plan to do it yourself or you plan to hire someone to do this grunt work for you, research is the key to successful penny stock trading.

The risks associated with penny stocks

Aside from the usual risks that come with trading volatile stocks, here are some things that you may not be aware of, even if you're not a complete beginner:

Spam: Everyone has seen it, and everyone despises it. As an investor, spam can be found not only in the inbox of your email, it can also be found in many places online. Penny stocks are not immune either. Scammers make a lot of money by promoting sketchy penny stocks to investors that may not know that this practice exists.

Be aware of dilution: Sometimes a company will need to issue additional stock in order to gain capital. When this happens, it usually leads to the dilution of the stock that is already held by its investors, meaning that the stock decreases in value. This is commonplace and is not considered to be shady dealings at all, but it is something that investors need to be aware of.

Here today and gone tomorrow: Pink sheets and the OTCBB do not have to meet minimum standard requirements to stay on the exchange. Minimum standards are in place to protect investors and as a guideline for companies issuing stock. When first starting out, you may want to stick with trading on a major exchange because they have regulations in place which protect you and your investment.

The short squeeze: This is a tricky, calculated situation where a very heavily shorted commodity or stock moves higher very sharply and makes the short sellers have to close out their short positions, which only adds to the stock's sudden upward pressure. The term 'short squeeze' refers to the fact that the short sellers are effectively being 'squeezed' out of their position in the stock, and typically at a loss.

Not enough available information or history: Penny stocks are known for the difficulty in finding information and history on them, which makes it even more difficult to make an informed decision when trading. If you paid enough attention to what worked for you and what didn't when you were paper trading and heed the warnings and advice of trusted sources such as this book, you will be able to make more informed decisions.

Watch out for the pump and dump: The most infamously common and widely used scam in the penny stock world is known as the pump and dump. It is used as the basis for other penny stock scams and is highly illegal, but still extremely common. Crooked analysts and brokers utilize misleading marketing ploys to artificially 'pump up' the price of a stock that they own to persuade inexperienced penny stock investors to purchase their stock.

When the inexperienced investors buy into the hype and the stock, this causes the share prices of that stock to rise, somewhat significantly. When the crooked party decides that their share price has risen sufficiently, they sell their own shares and make a huge profit. The kicker is that they are still promoting the stock to newbie penny stock investors and telling them how great of an investment it is at the same time they are selling off their stock. This type of insider selling forces the share price of that stock to fall rapidly and the inexperienced investor who is unaware of the scam is left holding stock that is absolutely worthless and they will end up losing their money on it.

It is very likely that you have or will come across a pump and dump scam through your email or other online avenues. In order to quickly promote their stock, pump and dump scams often use urgent hype phrases such as:
- "you don't want to miss this opportunity"
- "phenomenal growth"
- "hidden gem"
- "act now"

Pump and dump scams will never show you any actual analysis or management info, and if you ask for these things you will either be completely ignored, or someone will tell you that they don't have access to that information at that time or something like that. They are lying. They are wasting your time.

Chapter 7: Consider Options Trading

For those looking to take their level of interaction with the stock market to the next level, options trading is a great place to start as it will naturally allow you to support your existing investments as well. In many ways, options are just like bonds or stocks, which means they are securities which can be traded with the hopes of making a profit based on the direction the asset related to the security moves. Options differ from both stocks and bonds in that when you purchase one, you are purchasing the ability to choose whether or not you want to interact with the relevant asset at a specific price point for a specific length of time. This means that if the market doesn't behave as you expect it to, you have the ability to walk away while only losing a fraction of what you would if you had purchased the related asset directly.

While this may sound complicated, in reality, this same process is used every day when individuals who are interested in buying a home negotiate a price with a homeowner who is interested in selling their home and come to an agreement on a price, but then have to wait for the buyer's home loan from a bank to go through. Despite whatever changes the housing market might experience between the point the contract is signed and the point the loan is approved, the price in question is locked in as long as the buyer chooses to act on it. This means they could get a really good deal if the value of the home increases in the interim or they could walk away if the market suddenly drops the price significantly. Either way, the buyer is protected and has the option to what is right in the moment.

Putting options to work for you

Options are generally used in two main ways, as a form of speculation and as a form of insurance. Those who are interested in testing their knowledge of the market against its realities are typically interested in speculation which means they determine which direction the market is likely to move in a specified amount of time and they make money through proper trades if they are correct. Due to the specifics of options trading, as discussed below, it only takes a small change in any related asset prices to create massive losses or huge gains depending.

On the other hand, options can be used as a type of insurance on other, riskier investments as they can be purchased at the buy-in price for a risky underlying stock that you believe has the potential to either increase dramatically or decrease significantly. With the right option in place you can weather any uncertainty as if the bottom drops out from underneath the asset then you will still have a sale price that will at least prevent you from losing any investment capital in the interim.

You will also want to keep in mind the two main different types of options, European and American. Despite the names, the differences in the two come from the freedom purchasing an option gives the holder. American options can be exercised from the point they are purchased to the point they expire. Meanwhile, European options can only be exercised right at the moment they expire which makes them the riskier of the two by a fair margin. Both American and European options fall under the classification of vanilla options which means they have standard rates and time limits while exotic options can vary based on a wide variety of criteria which makes them best avoided by beginners.

Besides the options themselves, options traders are also classified based on their propensity to buy (holders) or sell (writers). Writers and holders then typically specialize in either puts or calls. In every trade, the holder will always have more power than the writer as if the holder decides to act on the option the writer has to sell, even if it isn't in their best interest to do so in the moment. Furthermore, if holders find themselves in a scenario where their plan doesn't appear to be coming together, they can then easily walk away and minimize their losses at the very least.

Know the lingo

When it comes to trading options effectively, one of the first things you are going to want to do is to familiarize yourself with the common terms that options traders are likely to use to ensure that even if you can't trade like a professional at least you can speak like one.

Strike Price: The price of a given underlying asset at the moment the option is purchased is called its strike price.

Exercised: When the movement of an underlying asset makes the specifications of a given option favorable then it is exercised or taken advantage of and the ownership of the underlying asset changes hands.

Trade out: If a holder exercises an option that the writer feels is not worth the current market value of the underlying asset then they can trade out which means they essentially buy back the holder's shares and relist them because they believe that a better deal is readily available even with the additional trouble taken into account. All told, some 50 percent of trades expire without any action being taken. Of the remaining 50 percent, only 10 percent are actually exercised with the remaining 40 percent ending up getting traded out.

Listing: The process of creating a new call is referred to as listing an option. Listed options appear on national exchanges and it is recommended that you only deal with listed options until you make it past your options trader novice phase. If you are dealing with vanilla options, then you can realistically expect all of the options you find to include 100 shares of the underlying stock in question.

In the money: If an option is currently in the money then the underlying stock that it is tied to is currently sitting at a point that is above whatever it is you initially paid for it. If, however, it is out of the money instead, then this means that it previously was in the money but has now dropped back down to a point where it is no longer profitable. If the underlying stock is exactly at the price at which you originally purchased it then the option can currently be thought of as at the money.

Biggest influences
Current stock price: When it comes to how the current stock price affects any related options, the two moves as expected, though there is not a 1 to 1 correlation between them. In general, as prices rise, the price of calls will as increase, and the price of puts will decrease, and the reverse will occur if the price of the underlying stock is decreasing.

Intrinsic Value: The intrinsic value is the amount of value that the underlying stock is guaranteed to keep, even while the time value continues to decrease over time. To determine the intrinsic value of a call option you can either divide the underlying stocks current price by that price after the strike price of the related call has been subtracted from it. Conversely, you can find the intrinsic value of a put option by subtracting the price of the put from the current stock price and then dividing that result by the current stock price.

The result, in either case, will be a reflection of the type of advantage that exercising the option in question would generate. Essentially, it can be seen as the minimum amount you will get from the option. For example, if there is a company whose stock is currently selling at roughly $34.80 then a call option of $30 would intrinsically be valued at $4.80 because $34.80-$30=$4.80. If this were a put option, then it would have no intrinsic value because $30-$34.80=-4.80 and a negative intrinsic value is inherently 0.

Time Value: The time value is related to the amount of time an option has left and can more effectively be thought of as the likelihood with which it is going to exceed the amount of its intrinsic value. To determine the time value for any option you simply take the price of the option in question and then subtract the amount of its intrinsic value. As a rule of thumb, expect your options to lose around 30 percent of its value in the first 50 percent of its time on the market with the other 70 percent decreasing over the remainder of its time.

For example, assume the option is then priced at $14. This would then mean that its premium is $4 more than its initial intrinsic value, which is where the time value comes into play. Time value is the added premium that is added to an existing option that represents how much time is left until expiration. The price of time is then influenced by various factors, including time until expiration, strike price, stock price, and interest rates. None of these, however, will ever be as significant to the price as implied volatility.

The implied volatility of a given underlying asset represents the overall expected volatility for the underlying asset across the entire life of the option. As the expectations for what the option might amount to before it expires change, the premium will react appropriately. Overall, the rise and fall of implied volatility will ultimately serve to determine the time value for a given option.

Option pricing models
Implied volatility can be determined using a variety of different option pricing models. In fact, it is the only factor in the model that can't be directly observed within the market itself. Instead, the option pricing model requires the use of additional factors to make it easier to determine the option's premium along with its implied volatility. You will find calculators for determining the results of these pricing models in your options trading platform

Black-Scholes pricing model: This formula, also known as the Black-Scholes-Merton pricing model, was the pricing model to be designed for option pricing. It is only effective with European options and it takes into account expected volatility, time to expiration, anticipated interest rates, strike price, asset price, and expected dividends. Created by a trio of economists in the 1970s, this pricing model accurately determines the values of derivatives.

Binomial model: The binomial pricing model uses a tree diagram that factors in volatility at every level to show traders all the possible paths the price of an option can take. It then works backwards to successfully determine the most likely price. The biggest benefit of this type of model is that you can use it to easily revisit any potential points of possibility, so you know the ideal strike price for any point prior to the option's expiration.

Chapter 8: Starter Option Trading Strategies

While jumping into the world of options trading can often mean absorbing quite a bit of information in a very short period of time; luckily, there are a number of simple strategies that new traders can use to improve their returns and decrease their relative amount of risk.

Buy/write: Sometimes referred to as the covered call, this strategy works when the trader purchases shares of an underlying stock while at the same time generating a call that is equal to the entire number of underlying stock shares owned. This strategy is ideal for traders who have already invested in the stock market and are looking for a way to shore up what may be previously questionable choices as the options will ensure that you are able to generate a premium even if the other bets placed in the investment don't exactly pay off. This is an especially viable way to ensure long term investments remain viable as the option will guarantee a profitable price for the length of its existence. This makes the covered call strategy ideal for LEAPs, index future and funds whose purchase was facilitated via margin.

Protective put: To get started using this strategy, the first thing you want to do is to purchase at least 100 shares of an underlying stock before generating an equal number of puts. If you are feeling bullish about the underlying stock price, then this is a great strategy as it will help you to keep losses in the short term to a minimum. A protective put is protective because it will help you to ensure that your short-term losses remain minimal by essentially creating a floor that ensures the price of the stock in question is only going to drop so far before being cut off by the put. This is one of the easiest mays to minimize market uncertainty overall which often makes it an attractive choice early on to new traders.

As a general rule, protective puts are less of risk than a put that is generated on its own which makes them an ideal place to test trading theories in the real world where the results are going to be controlled as much as possible. What's more, this strategy will also ensure that you always have spare shares available should something get exercised unexpectedly.

Covered call: Also known as the buy-write strategy, a covered call involves purchasing assets while at the same time writing a call on the assets being sold. In order for this strategy to work properly, you need to own the amount of the asset in question equal to the amount of assets in the call option you create. This is a great position to use if you have a separate position on the short term as well as an opinion that is neutral in regard to the assets in question and are also looking to generate a premium for bonus. This is also a good choice when it comes to protecting against a decline in the value of the asset in question. Covered calls can be used for LEAPS, index futures and on exchange traded funds that are bought on a margin.

Married Puts: In this type of strategy, you would purchase a set number of shares of a specific underlying stock before purchasing a put for the same number of shares. This is an ideal strategy to pursue if you are bullish regarding the price of the asset in question and are looking to prevent short term losses to their earnings. This is a good way to generate an artificial floor to brace against a drastic drop in price. While it is never beneficial to put money into a given asset with the assumption that it is going to collapse in the relatively near future, married puts are a great way to ensure existing investments against market uncertainties and minimizing uncertainty is always the right choice.

While not ideal in every scenario, if you take the time to use them sparingly, and in the right times you will find they are a powerful tool to your continued options trading success. It is important to always start every potential transaction with an expectation of the potential risk in question and then to factor in additional costs related to potential married puts accordingly.

Bull call spread: To use this strategy, you will want to start by purchasing a call option at a strike price you believe to be beneficial. You will then want to sell a similar number of calls at a higher strike price. Both calls should have the same underlying asset and the same timeframe. This is a useful strategy to use if you are bullish on the strength of the underlying asset in question and your research indicates that the price is likely to increase in the time frame you have chosen.

This strategy is also known as a vertical credit spread because it has a pair of mismatched legs. Legs that are sold close to the money generate a credit spread that typically contains a net credit along with a positive time value. On the other hand, a debit spread is created with a short option that ends further from the money than when it started. Overall, this strategy is considered a net buy.

Bear put spread: The bear put spread is similar to the bull call spread but is used in opposite circumstances. Specifically, you begin by purchasing a pair of put options, one at a higher strike price and another at a lower strike price. You are going to want to purchase an equal number of each and ensure that they have the same underlying asset and timeframe. This strategy is useful when you feel bearish on the underlying asset in question as it helps you limit your losses if you are incorrect about the way the market is moving. This strategy should be used cautiously, however, as your overall profits are going to be limited to the difference between the two puts you purchased minus the cost of any transaction fees.

The ideal time to use a bear put spread is if you are interested in short selling an underlying asset and using a more common put option doesn't seem to be the right choice. You will find them useful if you are interested in speculating that prices are on a downward trend and don't want to invest a larger amount of capital waiting for the worst to happen. When using a bear put spread you are literally planning for the worst while hoping for the best.

Protective collar: The protective collar strategy can be executed by buying into a put option that is already out of the money. From there, you will then want to write a secondary call option that is based on the same underlying asset and is also out of the money. This strategy is useful if you have already taken a long position on an underlying asset that has seen a number of strong gains in the recent past. Making use of a protective collar then allows you to ensure the current level of profit remains steady while also retaining control of the underlying asset should its positive trend continue.

Utilizing a protective collar is as easy as ensuring the contract for the put option you purchased was at a strike price that is more than likely enough to ensure you retain a majority of the profits you gained through the process. From there, you will be able to fund the collar strategy using the call option you have written as long as you are sure it relates to the specific Digit. This strategy is particularly useful as it allows you to easily maintain your profits while at the same time only increasing your additional costs a minimal amount. Furthermore, this is a great way to move funds about for tax purposes as any option that you roll over does not need to be accounted for until it has been either purchased or expired.

Straddle: This strategy is effective in a bullish or bearish market and can be used to either go long or short. The long straddle can be extremely effective if you feel as though the price of a given underlying asset is going to move significantly in one direction, you just don't know what direction that will ultimately be. To utilize this strategy, you will need to purchase a put and a call, both using the same underlying asset, strike price, and timeframe. After the long straddle has been created successfully you will be guaranteed to generate a profit if the price in question moves in either direction before it expires.

On the other hand, if you are interested in utilizing a short straddle, you will instead want to sell a call and a put with the same costs, timeframe and underlying asset. This will allow you to profit from the premium, even if everything else doesn't turn out as well as you may have liked. This guaranteed profit means that this is a particularly useful strategy if you don't expect to see movement very much in either direction before the option expires. Nevertheless, it is still important to remember that the chances that this strategy will be successful are directly related to the odds that the underlying asset is going to move in the first place.

Strangle: This strategy is effective in a bullish or bearish market as, functionally, a strangle is similar to a straddle except that it is often cheaper to execute on as you are buying into options that are already out of the money. As such, you can typically pay as much as 50 percent the cost of a straddle for a strangle which makes it even easier to play both sides of the fence. Typically, a long strangle is more useful than a short straddle because it offers up twice the premium for the same amount of risk.

To use the long strangle correctly, you will want to purchase a call along with a put that are both based on the same underlying asset with the same timeframe and different strike prices. The strike price for the call will need to be above the strike price for the put and both should be out of the money.

Spread (Butterfly): While all of the proceeding strategies have required pairs of options or specific positions, the butterfly spread takes things to another level by combining the bear and bull spread strategies to generate 3 different strike prices. To clarify, you start by purchasing a call as cheaply as you can while simultaneously selling 2 other calls related to the same underlying stock at a higher price and then selling a third call at the highest price of all. This will ensure that you are sure to find profits at numerous points in the life of the options as the underlying stock grows. This type of spread can also make it easier to profit when the market appears to be in a neutral phase.

The most effective time to use a butterfly spread is when you expect the underlying stock to increase but you are not sure by how much. The multiple strike prices ensure that you will see a profit as long as you are correct, and you don't have to worry about if you guess too low or too high. When deciding whether or not to utilize the butterfly spread it is important to only do so when the volatility of the underlying stock is relatively low as the higher the amount of volatility the higher the ultimate cost of the trade is going to be. The downside to the butterfly strategy is that you are going all in when it comes to betting that the underlying stock will move in a certain direction which means that if the trade turns sour you are out 3 times as much as normal.

Iron Condor: To utilize this strategy properly, you will want to hold a short position as well as a long position on a pair of strangle strategies in order to take full advantage of a market that moves very little. The pair of strangles you want to use should be comprised of a long and a short, both at outer strike length. Alternatively, you could have a pair of credit spreads, a call spread that is above the current market price and a put that is below the current price.

If you plan on using the iron condor it is important to only do so when it comes to indices options as they have enough volatility to generate profits but not enough to cause new traders to lose their shirts sooner than is prudent for the learning process. Additionally, it is important to avoid taking a total loss on an iron condor as the potential for loss in these situations is significantly greater than those with many of the other relatively safer strategies. If the market fluctuates as normal then you don't need to worry, if it begins to move strongly in one direction, it is important to be prepared and exit as needed to prevent greater losses.

Iron Butterfly: To utilize this strategy you need to create either a short straddle or a long straddle while at the same time purchasing (or selling) a strangle. While it may appear similar to the basic butterfly spread, this strategy actually uses both puts and calls instead of simply utilizing one or the other. In this case loss and profit are equally limited to a precise range that is set by the strike prices uses. This is a good time to use options that are out of the money to minimize personal risk as well as cost.

A proper iron butterfly should include a pair of options that are set at the mid strike point which creates either the short straddle or the long straddle based on the options being sold or purchased. The wings of the butterfly come from the pair of options at the lower and higher strike prices that are generated after the sale of the strangle in question. This, in turn, offsets the short or long positions which limits the amount of profit or loss you will ultimately see.

Stock repair strategy: This is a great strategy to employ if you have already purchased shares of stock that is optionable and are stuck in a situation where you are watching its value decline with no clear recourse to rectify the situation. If the stock, you purchased was non-actionable then all you would be able to do is hold onto it in hopes that things turn around or double down in hopes of turning a profit at a lower breakeven point. Luckily, with optionable stocks, you also have a third alternative.

As an example, consider that you started out with 100 shares of a stock that you purchased for $50 a piece only to watch them fall to the current price of $40 each. You are unwilling to invest anything else into this stock and are afraid to take any more downside risk. Once you are ready simply to break even then it is time to initiate the stock repair strategy.

To begin you would want to purchase a single 60-day call option on the stock at the $40 price point for $3 while also selling 2 60-day call options at $1.50. It is important to keep in mind that the spread won't cost you any credits or debits. This is because the cost of the calls you purchased at the rate of $3 per 100 shares for a total of $300, will be completely offset by the premium that is generated from the sale of the written calls at the rate of $1.50x2x100 for a total of $300.

The purchase of the $40 call will provide you with the opportunity to purchase another 100 shares at the $40 price point while the 2 $45 calls will mean that you have to sell 200 shares at $45 if you are assigned. While you currently only have 100 shares, you could exercise the $40 long call to generate the required extra shares and make $5 per share at a relative profit of $500 which would cover the assignment.

Chapter 9: Other Choices

Index Funds

When it comes to picking the ideal index fund for you to get started with, the first thing you will need to consider is the level of risk you are comfortable with, the length of time you plan on investing and your overall goals for the investment both short-term and long-term. Depending on the answer, you will then need to decide if you are looking for a mutual traded index fund or one that is exchange traded. If you aren't sure which is the right choice for you right now, consider the following:

- If all of your goals are long-term, then an index mutual fund is likely the best choice. You can often find local variations of this account that come with zero transaction fees.

- If you want something that is more active, then a fund that is exchange traded is typically the best choice as they are traded the same way you would trade stocks. This leaves you with more control overall as you have a say when it comes to entering specific trades as well as the limits you set as well. You will also have a greater overall variety to choose from as you won't be limited to just a single index.

Once you know what type of fund you are looking for, the next thing to do is to consider the expense ratio of the ones that catch your eye. Beyond that, you will also want to ensure that the fund you choose tracks the index in question successfully. To ensure this is the case, you will want to track the stocks the index tracks on your own and then match it to the index's performance to see how it stacks up.

It is also important to understand that just because an index might seem tempting, doesn't mean it is going to be the right choice for you, right now which means ensuring it matches your current investment objectives. If you are more interested in speculative growth, then an index with a small cap is a good choice. It is also important to understand that just because an index is said to minimize risk doesn't mean that it is completely devoid of risk as a result. Remember, indexes can be just as volatile as the market as a whole.

Retracement strategy: To properly implement this strategy, it is important that you are able to determine a likely pattern for the price of the stock to continue trending towards. To take advantage of this fact you wait for each price increase before the inevitable decrease which comes as some people sell and others try and trade the opposite. You sell on the high and use the profits to buy back in at an increase of shares under the assumption that it will rise again. Then you simply repeat until you are no longer sure of the increase.

This strategy will only work effectively when there is something major enough to cause ripples across the market that are not felt all at once. This strategy will become less effective the more unsure you are about additional jumps in price and should therefore always be used carefully. You may be tempted after seeing a single large jump from a stock to try and employee this strategy but beware of using it flippantly. Stay strong and you will turn a profit.

Reversal strategy: This strategy is best used when there is otherwise little going on in terms of market movement. The goal here is to find ideal price levels which will then be used to trade as soon as a price increase hit. These quick increases won't provide much in terms of substantial profitability but rather are used to take advantage of periods where there is not much trading going on. When implementing this strategy, it is important to be sure that there is no news about to break in a given field or even one that is adjacent to the field your stock is in as that can easily ruin your plans.

Consider ETFs

An ETF, or exchange-traded fund, is a marketable security that tracks a stock index, a commodity, bonds, or a basket of assets. Although similar in many ways, ETFs differ from mutual funds because shares trade like common stock on an exchange. The price of an ETF's shares will change throughout the day as they are bought and sold. The largest ETFs typically have higher average daily volume and lower fees than mutual fund shares which makes them an attractive alternative for individual investors.

While a majority of the ETFs on the market these days track stock indexes, there are also ETFs that invest in commodity markets, bonds, and other asset classes. Many ETFs even have the option for investors to use hedging, speculation or income strategies. Shareholders in an ETF each receive a portion of the profits in proportion to the number of shares they own. This means they are entitled to interest or dividends, and they may even earn residual value if the fund is liquidated.

Another benefit of the ETF is that it is more tax efficient than a mutual fund. This is due to the fact that the buying and selling that takes place does so via an exchange which means the ETF sponsor has no need of redeeming their shares each and every time an investor makes the choice to sell nor issue shares when a new investor wants to buy in. Likewise, redeeming shares from a specific fund can actually trigger a tax liability which means listing the shares via the exchange will also keep tax costs low. When it comes to a mutual fund, on the other hand, every time an investor sells their shares, they sell it back to the fund which means the shareholders of the fund must pay for the resulting tax penalty.

Pros and cons: ETFs also offer up a variety of benefits in addition to reasonable costs and an efficient tax dodge. In fact, simply by owning an EFT for an indexed stock, you receive all of the benefits of diversification that you get with an index fund along with the ability to short-sell and utilize margin to the fullest. Even if you only purchase a single share there are rarely any minimum deposits to worry about. What's more, some brokers will even off zero-commission trading on certain ETFs which makes it a great way to get in with very low risk.

However, it is also important to remember that no form of investing is without cost, which means that some will be better deals than others. Some may even offer a larger concentration of a specific stock or asset. After all, there are no guarantees that just because they have previously met expectations that they will continue to do so. This has led ETFs to play a major role in sudden crashes in the past, including serious market declines in February 2018, August 2015 and May 2010.

Swing trading

Generally speaking, swing trading is somewhere between day trading and not quite as long as investment trading as positions taken rarely last more than two week. With swing trading, the goal is to identify the overall trend the stock is likely to take and then capture gains within that trend.

Successful swing traders tend to work the main trend that a chart is presenting at any given time. There are also swing trading opportunities that manifest when a specific stock begins moving back and forth between support and resistance points and swing traders will take long positions when the price reaches the support level and short positions when it nears the resistance level.

Bullish trades: Due to the fact that stock market prices rarely move in a straight line, bullish swing traders typically need to look for initial upward movement as the primary part of a trend before expecting a reversal, otherwise known as a counter trend. Once this counter trend has successfully completed its arc, there should then be a resumption of upward movement. You will want to enter into a bullish swing trade only once the counter trend has ended and the uptrend has restarted.

With this out of the way, you should then be able to determine the ideal time to enter a specific trade by isolating the relevant movement of the counter trend. A good way to do this is by determining when the stock trades at a price that is higher than the previous high. The entry point that you should find will then most likely be comparable to the price point from the previous few days.

Bearish trades: While rarely as easy to predict as uptrends, downtrends tend to follow all the same patterns just in reverse. They will likely move in a downward pattern, hit a point of retracement, reverse and repeat. After this has happened several times, it will then be far easier to see. Throughout all of this time, it should be possible to see the bearish retracement and rallies forming as a counter trend.

Tactics that are useful when dealing with a positive trend will typically work with a negative trend as well. You will also still only want to enter into a bearish swing trade after it is clear that the downward movement is actually the trend.

Swing trading basics:

- Stick to large-cap stocks: When it comes to be a successful swing trader, it is impossible to do so without sticking to the right types of stocks. The best swing trade candidates are going to be those of the large-cap variety which tend to be those that see some of the most active trading across the major exchanges. Assuming the market is currently active, these stocks will then move between a pair of well-defined extremes which provides you, as a swing trader, with the opportunity to trade the trend in one direction and then back the other direction when the inevitable shift occurs.

- Know what to look for in the market: Generally speaking, when the market is at either extreme you will have a more difficult time swing trading for a prolonged period of time when compared to a market that is more moderate in nature. This is because when the market is at one extreme or another it is far rarer for even the most active of stocks to exhibit the same level of well-defined up and down movement that is more common when the market remains relatively stable for weeks or months at a time. When the market is stuck in bear or bull mode, momentum is far more likely to only move in one direction before dropping off, meaning that the ideal strategy is one that focuses on this longer-term directional trend.

- The exponential moving average is key: Simple moving averages provide support and resistance levels, as well as bullish and bearish patterns. Support and resistance levels can signal whether to buy a stock. Bullish and bearish crossover patterns signal price points where you should enter and exit stocks. Meanwhile, the exponential moving average is another variation that places additional importance on certain data points based on how recently they were created. The exponential moving average provides traders with a clear bead on the current trend as well as ideal exit and entry points.

Reconsider your broker: As you should never jump right into any type of trading trading without having a good grasp on the basics of stock market investing, you likely already have a broker that you have been using for some time. The first thing that you will need to do before you start trading more accurately is to ensure that your broker will suit your new, and much more demanding needs. If you wait until you already feel as though you are missing out on profits to find a new broker then the damage has already done which is why it is better to look at this core facet of your trading business under a microscope, the sooner the better.

In order to find the right broker for your new day trader trading method the first thing that you will want to do is determine what features, if any, the broker that you settle on absolutely has to have no matter what. While most traders won't have their own set of requirements, those with special needs will do well to consider them first and foremost. With the basics in mind, the next thing that you will need to do is start researching various options. First and foremost, you are going to need to consider the fees that are placed on each individual trade as your overall trade amount is often going to be quite high. These fees can come about not just as a result of the commissions on trades but also on things like data fees, platforms fees, withdrawal fees, and inactivity fees.

Additionally, many brokers place additional limitations that individuals must meet if they plan on day trading, including significantly increased minimum balance amounts or proof of general trading competency to prevent themselves from appearing to take advantage of the ill-informed. Finally, you will need to know what the margins are like if you are day trading in the futures market or what levels of leverage are available in the stock market as well as the forex market.

Day Trading
Broadly defined as buying and selling the same security in a single day, day trading is most common in both the forex and stock markets. Armed with a large amount of data, and an even larger bank roll, the best day traders take advantage of high amounts of leverage as well as strategies

for success that come to fruition in the short term to make large sums from price movements that are otherwise relatively minor.

The act of day trading is one that is hotly debated these days, simply because like many ways of making large amounts of money in short periods of time it is easy for the uniformed to jump in blindly and lose their shirts before they have even properly gotten started. The truth of the matter is that day trading is like any other type of investment, never without risk but certainly far from random. Unlike traditional investing, day trading is much more of an active full-time job rather than a relatively passive way to make extra money on the side. If you hope to succeed in the long term when it comes to day trading, then you need to be willing to put in the time and effort to be successful day in and day out. Essentially, if you are trading in a normal fashion then what you are really doing is investing.

What this means is that even if you are confident when it comes to picking stocks or forex pairs, the lessons that you have learned over the years no longer apply. Day trading is its own beast entirely and that comes with its own set of strengths as well as weaknesses. While on one hand, you never have to worry about how any of your trades are going to look in the long term, on the other hand, you are never going to be able to wait for your trades to stabilize if things head sideways more quickly than you had initially hoped.

Day traders are constantly scanning the 60-minute, 30 minute, 10 minute, 5 minute and 1 minute charts trying to find the right investment for the right moment to jump on a potentially lucrative opportunity to present itself. From there it is about identifying the right opportunities, finding a trade that fits their plan and sitting on it until just before it becomes unprofitable and repeating with enough accuracy that they end up coming out ahead more often than not.

As a new day trader, it is important to keep in mind that more often than not, in this case, is going to be a little more than 50 percent of the time, and only if you are very good at trading in these short time frames. Additionally, you will often hold trades for just a matter of minutes before selling based on the subtlest of movements in either direction.

Day trading difficulties: With so much on the line in such a short period of time it is important to have a clear idea of the various types of difficulties you may face when it comes to getting your feet wet in the world of day trading.

- Commissions limit profits: Day traders have a much higher overall trade volume than other types of traders which naturally means that their expenses in this arena are going to be much higher than other types of traders. While there are ways to minimize these costs, there is no denying that day trading is not for those with a smaller overall bankroll.

- Discipline is of the upmost importance: When it comes to day trading successfully, being able to stick with your trading plan, even in the midst of emotional turmoil, is of the upmost importance. This attribute is prized in this scenario simply because it is so easy to misstep and wipe out a day's hard work in a matter of seconds.

Day trading professionally: When it comes to day trading as a profession, day traders are classified in one of two ways, those who are lone traders and those who trade for large firms. The traders who work for larger institutions are typically going to have access to a wide variety of tools that other traders can only dream of. This high degree of access means that they can focus on trades that are going to generate an easy profit as they will have access to information the second it becomes public allowing them to act on it while lone traders are still confirming the information they have received.

On the other hand, lone day traders are going to be much more well-equipped than the average small-time investor, otherwise, they are not going to be able to compete with other lone traders on an even playing field. They are often looking for the same types of trades as those traders who work for large firms, but their more limited resources mean that they are almost always going to need to take a greater degree of risk to achieve the same level of results.

First hour trading: While it is not hard to find day traders who are content to flit into and out of the market all day, every day, the real truth is the two periods of the day during which trade volume is the greatest are during the first hour of the day and again during the last hour of the day. What this means is that if you confine yourself to only trading during the first hour of the day you cannot only make things much easier on yourself overall but can still make a profit as well. Analysts have proven that the market only continues to make good on early trends roughly 20 percent of the time which means that 80 percent of the time you have nothing to lose with this method while gaining an entire day in the process.

As long as you take the following process to heart, you will find that you will be able to create enough liquidity during this time period that you will be able to jump in and out when the market is just starting to solidify, making a profit in the process. In order to employ this type of strategy successfully, you are going to need to have access to the funds to generate a high volume of orders in a short period of time if you hope to be successful. Experts agree that this type of strategy will only work for those who have $100,000 or more on hand to get started with.

- Initial 5 minutes: The most common day trader chart is the 5-minute chart and it will be the first one you should concern yourself with as well. The first 5 minutes will provide you with a wide variety of information that is crucial to making an informed decision later on including determining the various price or volume gaps that certain stocks are likely to develop based on the news that has occurred while the market was closed. The best way to get a jump on these details is to have a clear idea of what the news is likely to bring for the day including any rumored announcements or scheduled reports.

- While you are going to want to watch this period of time quite closely, it is important to only look and to never touch. The first 5 minutes is without a doubt one of the most volatile of the entire day and getting into the market at this point is little better than gambling. Take note of the start of any potential trends but avoid making a commitment until things have fully shaken out a little more.

- 9:30 to 9:50: While not a segment that you are going to see getting discussed very often, there are plenty of reasons to consider this timeframe as opposed to waiting for the additional details that will reveal themselves by 10 am. First and foremost, getting in at this time will provide you with a lack of competition as you will be able to move before those who are watching the 15-minute and 30-minute charts while at the same time only taking on relatively little additional risk. This is the period when it is crucial that you work out what the low and high values for the morning are actually going to be as otherwise it will be difficult to set boundaries for the trades you are currently considering. This period should provide sign posts that should point you towards trends that you would do well to take advantage of.

- 9:50 to 10:10: Depending on the results of the previous 20 minutes you will want to make a more confident move during this time period, either trading with or against the trend based on the indicators that you have seen. If you are planning to take advantage of this trading strategy, then this is the timeframe during which you will want to consider placing all of your trades for the day as if you wait even an extra 5 minutes then you will no longer be ahead of the pack and as a result your overall profits for the day will be seriously hampered because of it.

- 10:10 to 10:30: During this period, you are going to want to keep a close eye on your trades to ensure that the trends you were noticing early on continue on to maturity. While this might not seem like a long time to make a day's worth of profit, the truth of the matter is that if you got in by 9:50 am then you will have nearly a full hour to generate a profit using this timetable. What's more, if things are still proceeding smoothly then you can even hold out until 11 am, but only if the trends you predicted are proving exceedingly strong. During these instances, you will want to be ready to get rid of your holdings at a moment's notice if you want to prevent your profits from suddenly tilting in the opposite direction.

- Despite the fact that if things are going well you won't have much to do during this period, it is important to never approach it in a manner that can be described as lackadaisical. You never know when the moment that things start moving the other direction is going to arrive which means you need to be ready and waiting for it when it does. It is important to have a clear exit point in mind going into this time frame and to never get greedy. The levels of movement that you will be working with in this instance are going to be incredibly small which means that if you so much as get up to use the restroom without closing out then you risk ruining all of your hard work. Don't throw it all away now, remain laser focused until you have finished the day's work.

Chapter 10: What the master's Tell Us

Warren Buffet's Style of Investing

There are some things worth noting when it comes to Warren Buffet's style of investing. He utilizes more of a concentrated and qualitative approach when he places his stocks, which is similar to Graham who many consider to be his mentor. Warren favors the quality enterprises, which have good valuations and the ability to achieve a high level of growth. In guiding him with his decisions, Buffet uses investing tenets in different areas of business and management. They may look a bit cliché and easy, but they can be hard to implement. In the event that one particular tenet asks if the management is candid with the shareholders, this would not be the easiest thing to answer. On the other hand, there are particular examples of the reverse. Some of the concepts, which seem complex, are easier to implement like the 'Economic Value Added'.

Business tenets: Mr. Buffet places restrictions on what he terms as the circle of competence. The businesses that he is familiar with or the ones that he understands are the ones that he is most likely to invest in. He considers a deep understanding of the enterprises to be one of the most significant needs so that he can be able to accurately predict their business performances in the future. According to him, if you are not able to predict or understand the business, then it would not be impossible to give a projection on the performance.

A great example would be the tech boom and bust that came about during the turn of the century. Warren was not a fan of the dot com companies that were coming up, neither was he sufficiently acquainted with the companies to a level where he thought he could invest and in doing so, he chose to stay away. That is why he did not get so hurt when the tech bubble burst in the first few years of the 2000s. There are several firms which had knowledge of the tech industry and these were the ones that pulled out before the market dropped. However, the others who were so excited by the prospect of internet firms without first researching the field were the ones that got seriously hurt.

The business tenets of Buffet support the objectives of producing a strong projection of the stocks which are to be considered. The first thing is to analyze the business and not the market or even the economy at the time or what other investors are saying about the stock considering they have vested interest or not. The next thing is to look for a consistent operating history of the company. Warren then says to use that information in order to evaluate if the business has favorable prospects for the long-term or not.

Financial measure tenets: As implied before, Warren Buffet follows the value investor model for stocks. There are particular indicators and financial measures that he looks for in every corporation behind the stocks he opts for. These should be adopted by everyone that wants to consider a stock as well. Buffet has a preference for the return on equity measure as opposed to the earnings per share which many would consider as the primary deciding factor. Students of finance know though that return on equity as an indicator can be manipulated by the leverage which is a debt ratio and so it is a bit inferior to the returns on capital. In this case, the return on capital is more like the return on assets. Here, the numerator is the earnings attained for each capital provider and the denominator is inclusive of the debt and equity contributed via the business. Buffet has knowledge of this though instead examines the leverage in a separate manner preferring the low leverage type of firms and he looks for the high profit margins.

The first thing Buffet considers is what he terms as the owner's earnings that is basically the cash flow attained by the shareholders or just the cash flow to the equity. He terms it as the net income added to the amortization minus the expenditures of capital and the additional working capital. The sticklers will claim the particular adjustments, though this equation is close to the EVA before deducting an equity charge for the shareholding party. In the ultimate case with owners' earnings, Buffet considers the ability of the firm in generating cash for shareholders that are the residual owners.

Management tenets: His three management tenets are what Buffet utilizes in order to verify the quality of management of investments. This may be a very introspective question to ask from investing parties and it considers some of the following. Buffet asks if the management is rational. To be more specific, he asks if the management knows enough about the situation for it to make a reinvestment of the earnings or whether it is a better idea to return the profits to the shareholders in the form of dividends.

This question is quite profound as a lot of the related research is of the implication that historically as a group, the management would tend to be greedy and retain profits considering would want to still build an empire and seek scale as opposed to utilizing the cash flow in a way which would maximize the value of the shareholder. The other tenet which examines the honesty of the management is whether they reveal that mistakes can be made.

There is a question as to whether the management also resists the institutional imperative. This particular factor considers management teams which resist operating and the lemming sort of duplication of the competing strategies and particular tactics. It would be worth savoring considering it needs one to draw a line between parameters such as the duplication of the strategy of competitors and outmaneuvering those firms which are the first to market.

Value tenets: Warren Buffet especially tries to ascertain the intrinsic value of the firm and projects the future earnings of the owner and discounts them to the present. Though if have applied the other tenets, then the projection of the earnings in the future becomes that much easier as the returns become easier to predict. Warren ignores the volatility of the short-term usually and focuses on the returns of the long-term. He only acts when it comes to long-term fluctuations when considering a good deal.

In the event that the company seems to be good at $100 per share and then drops to a level of 90 dollars a share, then it would not be a surprise for him to pick up the additional shares at a discount. He also came up with 'moat' as a financial star to be short for the economic moat. This is what gives the firm a clear advantage over the others within the same industry or market and protects it from the competition.

At the end of the day, his tenets are what constitute a foundation when it comes to value investing or they are what others use as directives for this approach. It is an open query as to the level the tenets need modification in the future where consistent operating histories happen to be that much harder to find. Practically, everyone within the stock market wants to be the next Warren Buffet, though it is only a few who have been able to even imitate the success that he has had with trades. Even he suggests that small investors need to buy a low-cost index fund as opposed to individual stocks. His approach seems to be that of caution and safety more than anything else.

Stock Strategies from Livermore
Livermore has a belief that a stock would move in a particular direction, then you ought to enter the trade early enough after the indications from the market confirmed your judgment. As such, Livermore had the preference of trading those stocks whose prices were moving in an obvious trend. He had no interest in the stocks that illustrated small changes in their pricing with no strong trend. The patterns that he wanted to identify were those patterns which were in the pricing of the stock. Some of the traders at the present and during his time plotted the pricing and volume against the time on the charts. Though Livermore was not a fan of using the chart, but rather preferred the numbers.

Determining if the stock is in the bullish or bearish trend:
Livermore asserted he didn't begin as an expert until the point when he began foreseeing a portion of the significant

developments in the market. One of the advantages with regards to trading stocks is you may utilize a more extensive economic cycle and condition in order to foresee in the event that they will rise or decay. There are various measurable definitions on what constitutes the bullish trend or market rather than the bearish trend.

The dealers may likewise consider the basics in the economy in order to affirm if the bearish or bullish cycle is in play. It could be the least demanding methodology would utilize basic specialized examinations of the stock record with the most significant of the majority of the worldwide stock indices being over the 200 proportional, so a bullish market can be named with the opposite of meaning a bearish trend.

Then again, you might need to consider whether two months close above or under the year moving normal with the end goal to determine the equivalent. When trading utilizing the methodology instituted by Livermore, then you just go long when there is a bullish trend and short the market when there is a bearish trend.

Selection of particular sectors: At the point when the merchant starts going long or even short, then they need to choose the stocks that would be the best to buy. Stock indices might be obtained yet the profits can be boosted through picking the alluring stocks within the coming cycle. This would be better achieved with the utilization of the best down methodology which would consider the area indices that are distributed by any number of monetary administration stages.

Concentrating on the economic situations of that specific division might be without a doubt a major help. Actually, one may consider the costs of the part indices with the end goal to check whether they are additionally as bullish or bearish as the more extensive market file which would be an affirmation that you are considering the fitting division or industry.

Preparation to open the new trades when the new bear or bull trend starts.

Livermore guaranteed it was the stock dealer's errand in order to begin buying stocks from the beginning of the bullish market and hold to the trend till the positively trending business sector was doused or to begin shorting the stocks toward the start of the bear trend with indistinguishable guideline from with the buyer advertise. Livermore likewise suggested that at times, the market may not be bullish and not extremely bearish which is to state the time had come to escape the current exchanges, however, it would not be time to open a portion of the new ones of every contrary heading.

Stock selection: Livermore exchanged a portion of the two most smoking stocks from each chosen segment he needed to be in. One of the specialized methods for seeing the stocks influencing the most grounded highs or lows can be used, notwithstanding considering the money related information of the organizations are also a piece of the pie and different items. There happen to be two significant focal points of being within the best stocks in a specific division. The first would be the advantages that accompanied enhancement and the other thing Livermore saw that in the event that one of the stocks began fairing severely or more terrible than the other, then it was a sign there was a major issue with the specific company and when this happened, then it would be a sign to pull out from the specific stock.

One of the significant things with regards to trading stocks with the utilization of the Livermore approach would center the primary organizations which are stock heading the mechanical change and related client request. Livermore considered a ton amid his initial vocation and concentrated a lot of it on railroads, steel, and sugar which were a portion of the principle parts of the economic changes occurring amid the nineteenth century. Amid the current bull cycle, the specific thing is he would purchase forcefully from say, Apple in a similar way that he purchased sugar when new innovation was being started with the end goal to make the sugar reasonable.

Initiating the trade: Livermore was an expert at breakouts and moving on the breakdowns. He scaled into the new exchanges and not in an equivalent position size. Say Livermore found the beginning of a bullish trend or market. At that point, he would have an enthusiasm for specific stocks whether they are A or B within division C. Stock A could make another more expensive rate than it had been for various weeks or months.

At that point, he would buy the principal stock yet just with one fourth of the aggregate shares in that stock that he would purchase. At that point, he would attempt to see the way in which it acted. If it kept on rising firmly and make new highs, then he would begin purchasing again on a large portion of the rest of the quarters and afterward sit tight for additional time.

If the example continued, then he would purchase the rest of the shares he needed. He would have possessed the capacity to utilize a 1 percent expansion in the pricing as a signal which would be utilized to add to the exchange. If the move appeared not to be succeeding, then Livermore would quit. Through scaling into the exchange, he began to shield himself from an extreme lose when he was wrong about the manner in which the move was going.

Sitting pretty: One of the favored statements that Livermore has was that he profited when he was unwinding than he at any point did while moving. The suggestion was that there was nobody ever who could predict the market swings, so one ought to get it toward the beginning and not get out up to the time that the market has played out. Along these lines, they may purchase a stock for $10 and after that move, two years after the fact toward the finish of a bullish trend and after that make a profit which may even be more than 2000 percent of the vital.

He especially cautioned about moving on the pullbacks as a result of the dread market would have an inversion and after that endeavoring to buy the stocks at a later time when the misstep has been figured out. He admitted that he experienced this terrified thinking amid the beginning of trading before he picked up understanding and certainty.

Stock strategies from Benjamin Graham

Graham started through looking for potentially good investors who had above average intelligence through defining the action as investing as an operation, which on good analysis promises security of the principal and an adequate level of return. The activities, which did not meet the aforementioned prerequisites, are the ones, which are termed as speculative.

For Graham, the trading of bonds, stocks, or other investible assets would be investing only in the case where it is based on thorough analysis, promises safety of the principal, or would be expected to provide an adequate return. If not, then it would just be considered as speculation, which is highly discouraged according to Graham.

Investors play the part of owners: Graham encouraged the owners to view the stocks as reflecting on part of their ownership within the enterprise. He gave advice to the investors, so they could value their stock at that the potential buyer would be willing to pay for the business in order for it to be a going concern. This is important as an insight.

Too many of the investing parties consider the stocks to be certificates, which trade on the market for a particular price, which they are of the hope, is going to increase. The viewing of stocks as representing part of the ownership within the enterprise restructures the focus from the fluctuation's day to day to the factors which would otherwise drive the valuations, and which would be the fundamentals over the long-term.

Average long-term earnings: Graham has the idea that investors need to largely ignore any one of the quarters or the reported earnings of the year. The transitory factors in this case often led the numbers to vary in a significant manner depending on the period. In the same way, they could have been underrepresented in the underlying values. The average earnings over a number of years could have a declining effect on the individual year particular factors.

As such, the long-term trend when it comes to the average earnings would probably be more representative of the underlying intrinsic valuations. Graham also implied caution to investors so the earnings pro forma would not fool them. The diluted earnings set by the generally accepted accounting principles would have a low likelihood of being deceived. His focus on the average earnings over the longer term led to the adjusted price earnings concept.

Net-Nets: One of his favorite stocks having desired the margin of safety is termed as the net-nets. In order to find one of these, one starts with the current assets value in the organization and one minus the total amount of the long-term and the short-term debt. Then dividing the net level by the number of shares outstanding is going to result in the net current assets per share.

In the event the price of the stock is below the resultant number, Graham termed the stock as one of these net-nets. These stock prices would be less than the net current assets per share ignoring the value that is set to the long-term assets. Any person who was able to purchase the net shares of the net-net at the current price would be able to utilize the revenue from the liquidation of their current assets, so they would be able to pay the debts of the firm.

The purchaser would then be able to own the long-term assets at no price at all. It was the recommendation of Graham to assemble a diverse type of portfolio for these stocks and to wait for the market in order for their value to be realized. This strategy worked especially well when the net-net stocks were there in mass. However, as Graham noted a lot of the time, the market is not in one's pocket so to speak. The net-nets could be there when the overall market is declining but they may be rare when the market is on a boom. It is not wise to rely on the strategy of the net-net over the course of time.

Mr. Market: Graham came up with an imaginary persona which was known as Mr. Market to illustrate the random nature of the fluctuations within the pricing of various stocks. A lot of the time, the price of Mr. Market would be an estimate for the actual or underlying value. Some of the other times, he would offer to pay a price, which was excessive or sells a lot for too little of the price. Graham encouraged the investing parties to ignore the offerings of Mr. Market when it came to buying or selling for the majority of scenarios.

Overall, Benjamin Graham gave a large amount of investment guidance in his books and much of that information has been covered in the above text. It has been four decades since he last opened on investing, though his wisdom looks to be just as relevant for the market today as when it was first printed.

Stock Strategies from Seykota
Ed Seykota came up with the initial computerized trading system to trade some of the commercial accounts within the futures markets. After a hard time agreeing with management that had the ability to override signals as provided within the system in the interests of generating commissions, he opted to go solo. Seykota followed a

mechanical trend following the trader that constructed a majority of his systems around the exponential moving averages with a bit of reliance on pattern recognition. As such, the basic principle, which comes to mind behind trend following would ride the winners and cut the losers, though it would be easier said than done.

Technical analysis has always been the forte of Seykota. He claims that he thrives on three components within his trading style and these would be the current chart patterns, long-term trends, and identifying the right spots to buy and sell. These are what make up the basic when it comes to analysis. Seykota places a lot of emphasis on putting protective stops the minute he enters a trade and takes profits in the event the market goes wild.

Seykota says that keeping the bets manageable and small is going to assist with keeping one's emotions in tow. Without that, fear and greed may take over. The advice he gives is to speculate with less than 10 percent of the liquid net worth of the trader. Over the years, Seykota then shifted focus to the psychological parts when it came to trading. In the early nineties, he established a group where he would work with traders in order to bridge methods that curbed certain emotions in trading.

Stock Strategies from George Soros

As one considered a maverick hedge fund manager, Soros created significant annual returns after management fees. In spite of the animosity, which was generated through what would be considered adverse trading tactics and his investment philosophy, Soros spent decades at the head of the class among the elite investors.

Soros has come to be known as a short-term speculator. His philosophy entails making large high advantage type of bets in the direction of the financial markets. His hedge fund, global macro strategies concentrated on making big one-way bets on the movement of the currency rates, stocks, bonds, and other commodity rates based on particular macroeconomic analysis. As such, Soros bet that the value of certain factors within the economy of choice would either rise or fall.

This form of trading by the seat of one's pants was based on research but mostly executed on instinct. He studied the stocks of interest and let the movements of different financial markets and their participants be the ones that dictated the manner that he traded. He referred to the philosophy behind the way he traded as reflexivity. The theory eschews on the traditional ideologies of an environment based on equilibrium, where the information is revealed to all the participants in the market and they are able to affect the market fundamentals and their irrational behavior would lead to the boom and busts, which present particular investment opportunities.

The housing prices provide a good example of the theory implemented. When the lenders make it that much easier to attain loans, more people decide to go to the banks in order to revenue. With their revenue in hand, they opt to buy homes, and these increases the demand of the homes. According to basic economic theory, an increase in demand is an increase in the pricing. The higher prices then encourage the lenders to give more revenue.

More revenue within the hands of the borrowers means an increase in the rising demand for the homes and that means an upward spiraling cycle, which is housing prices that have been bid upwards past what the economic fundamentals would suggest is the reasonable rate. The way the buyers and lenders operate has had a big impact on the pricing of this commodity. An investment, which is according to the idea of the housing market, is going to eventually decline and crash is a typical Soros bet. He would in this scenario, short sell the shares of the major housing lenders as he depends on the housing boom going bust.

Developing an investing thesis according to the scientific method
One of the best lessons from Soros is for the investing parties to go along with his application of the scientific method. He utilizes several resources so that he can come up with a thesis on how equity needs to behave in particular market conditions. That is to say, that the investing thesis you use into your trades needs to be testable. If the market posits a bull approach, then a chart analysis should give all of the hints that this will be the case.

Before investing, you also need to consider the counterarguments
Prior to making any big investment decisions, Soros advocates that you do a lot of consulting much the way he does, and this may entail listening to contrary opinions. After listening to their input, Soros took his time to consider opinions and so reflect on his investing hypothesis. In doing so, no matter how rock solid the

investing thesis could be, there is always the chance that it is not the right way to go about it. Listening and digesting the other side of the argument is going to allow for one to consider every possible angle and see if you still like the idea before investing tangible funds.

Have a willingness to cut your losses: Through having a well-defined measurable success in mind before investing, Soros claims he is in a better position to assess if an investment is not going the way it should. In fact, he claims he even relies on instinctual or physical cues such as headaches or body pains, which he claims are a sign for one to cut his losses.

As such, the sales data has fallen short of different expectations and has caused the shares to fall from their highs. In this scenario, the investing parties would have attained benefits from cutting their losses based on the initial sales, which did not support the thesis. Overall, the market may not always be rational, though that is not indicative that one has to invest in an irrational manner.

Having a set of investing guidelines is going to best the emotionally charged purchases over the longer term. Though the approach by Soros when it comes to investing may not be the best thing for everyone, there is a particular internal logic to it, which is harder to ignore. In short, one ought to base their decisions to buy or sell according to a well-honed thesis, which has a number of verifiable results.

Chapter 11: Taxes

If you are a frequent trader, then you are very familiar with the mountain of taxes that come with stock trading. If you are new at this, you should know that if you do not manage your stock trading before tax season, the IRS will most definitely harvest your profits. In the end, if you ignore the aftermath of taxes that come with stock market trading, you will end up with much fewer returns and probably give up of stock trading altogether. There are two main ways that you can be taxed while trading in the stock market.

Through qualified retirement accounts: This is a type of plan that is in accordance with the regulations of Internal Revenue Code Section 401 (a). It makes it qualified to receive specific tax benefits. This is a retirement plan that is established by the employer in order to benefit the employees and workers of the corporation. This type of account gives your money the time to grow tax-free until you withdraw it. It also allows you to invest your capital before you pay your income taxes.

Qualified plans give an employee the freedom to defer some part of their income into the plan, which reduces the employees' present-day income tax liability. This also reduces the amount of income that is eligible for tax. To be simple, this type of plan is designed to make the employee want to work for the company and allows the company to keep good employees. These types of accounts lower your tax bill and you only pay regular income taxes on your earnings and contributors when you withdraw money in retirement. For example, the Roth retirement account gives you the freedom to invest after tax dollars. However, it does not lower your present tax bill. You can also withdraw earnings and contributions tax-free when you retire.

There are two main types of qualified retirement account plans. First is the defined benefit plan, which provides employees a determined pay, which in turn shifts the risk to the employer in order to invest and save so that you can meet plan liabilities. An example of this is a traditional annuity-type pension. The second is under defined contribution plans.

For these, the amount that employees receive in retirement is dependent on how much they save and invest on their own during the time that they are working or remain employed. A 401(k) is one of the most popular examples of this. Other examples of qualified retirement accounts include 403(b) plans, Simplified Employee Pension (SEP), Target Benefit Plans, Employee Stock Ownership (ESOP) plans, and Money Purchase Plans.

So when should you participate in qualified retirement accounts? If you think that during your retirement you will be in a lower tax bracket, then you should stick to a regular account. However, if you think that you will be in a higher tax bracket, then you should consider getting a qualified retirement account. Of course, you should always consult before making any big decisions.

Unqualified stock investment: Unqualified stock investment is a retirement plan that is completely sponsored by the employer. It does, however, fall outside of the employee retirement income security act guidelines.

This type of plans is designed to meet specific retirement needs for company executives and other specific employees. These plans are exempted from the discriminatory and top-heavy testing that normally qualified plans are subject to. Generally, with unqualified stock investment, you have two types of basic taxes to keep in mind.

First, if the stock you have invested in is eligible for paying dividends, then you are eligible to pay income taxes on the payments. The tax of dividends is usually 15 percent, but it is subject to change depending on the stock market and economy. If you hold on to the stock for more than one year, any gain you receive from it is taxed under long-term capital gains rates.

However, if you sell stock for a profit, stock that you have owned for more than a year, then you will pay regular income taxes on the gain you make. This could be higher than 15 percent depending on the tax bracket you belong to. It is always advisable to check with your advisor in order to prepare accordingly. So, what happens when you sell for a loss? For most cases, you can claim both a long and short-term capital loss. These losses are not all bad as they can be used to offset capital gains.

Before you decide, therefore, it is important that you consider the consequences of your stock investments. The general rule is that the more you can put into a qualified retirement account, then the better it is from a tax point of view. Always check with a qualified tax advisor before making any decisions.

Managing taxes while trading: Most of the time, taxing in the stock market is heavily dependent on your personal situation. However, this is not all it depends on. There are some few simple principles and tax tips that can be applied to most trading situations, which can help you save money. In the next section, you will explore some of these tips, which will help you make smart decisions and save you a lot of money.

Dividends: If you are a frequent trader, then you probably end up paying a lot of capital gains tax when you decide to trade your mutual fund shares because you forgot or decided to overlook dividends that you reinvested in the fund for a long period of time. When you increase your investment in a fund, you will reduce the amount that is eligible for tax.

This only works for reinvested dividends. For example, let us say that you originally invested 10,000 dollars in a mutual fund and dividends of 2,000 dollars reinvested in additional shares over the years. To continue, you would sell your stake in the fund for 15,000 dollars. This would make your taxable gain calculated by subtracting the original 10,000-dollar investment and the 2,000 dollar reinvestment from the 15,000 dollar sale. Therefore, your taxable gain would be 3,000 dollars. Most people usually forget to remove their reinvested dividends and would end up paying a hefty 5,000 dollars.

Though, this example does not present a reduction in taxable income as a big deal. If you do not succeed in taking advantage of this possibility could eventually cost, you a lot of money as time goes by. Imagine an extra 2,000 dollars every tax season because you failed to consider dividends every year. You end up with tax-adjusted returns that will have you suffering in the end.

To actively take advantage of this rule, ensure that you keep well-detailed records of your invested dividends and also examine the rules of taxes that can be applied to your situation when tax season comes along. Through doing this, you will always remember to use details to your advantage. Also, you will be well-studied up on tax avoidance opportunities and use them to your advantage.

Bonds: When your favorite brand of ice cream fails to give you the satisfaction that you desire, you end up seeking refuge in another brand hoping to receive at least a cushioning place until you can find the next big flavor or type. Likewise, when the stock market performs badly, investors go to find a place to put all their money until the stock market is back up. These safe cushions are bonds. They regularly perform counter to equities and what is more, give interest income. The best part is that you may not be required to pay tax on all the interest that you received.

So how do you achieve this? Most bonds pay out semi-annually (twice a year). Therefore, if you buy bonds in between the interest payments, you will not be required to pay tax on the interest that you acquired before you bought the bonds. Of course, you are obliged to report the entire amount that you received but you will be allowed to remove the gathered amount on a different line.

Other safe harbors include short-term government debt and for the retail investor, municipal bonds are major harbors of tax advantages. It is the duty of the government and state municipalities to issue out municipal bonds. They issue them out for the benefit of people such as building a hospital or matching required expenses. Many municipal bonds are issued with the tax-exempt status, which in turn means that the interest that they generate is not necessarily claimable when your file tax returns. The ones that are highly rated are low-risk and also the ones that will attract you.

Write-Offs: If you bought, for example, a computer for your home last year, then it is possible to write off part of what the computer cost you, but only if you used the computer to help manage your portfolio and place trades. The deductible amount is dependent on how often you used the computer to help you with managing your investments. For example, if you bought the computer at 2000 dollars and you used it 25 percent of the time to monitor your investments, then 500 dollars is technically an expense that can be written off as part of the expenses for buying the computer.

People who invest in small businesses and/or are self-employed often have to face many business operation expenses that qualify to be write-offs. For example, if you travel for business, which requires you to look and pay for accommodation, then the cost of your accommodation and meals you got there can be written off as a business expense. This is all bound by specific limits that are often depended on where it is you travel to. If you travel a lot and forget to put in these personal expenses, then you will end up losing a sizable amount of money.

If you are a homeowner and you have moved and sold your home within the year, then you should consider the actual amount you had to give during the process of buying the house when you report the capital gain of selling the house. This is also eligible if you decided to renovate the house you have used or has been in use for more than one year. You can include the cost of making these renovations into the adjusted cost base of the house. This, in turn, cuts the capital gain that is faced when you sell the house.

Add Broker Fees to Stock Cost: As you may already know, buying stocks is not a free transaction. You will always have to pay commissions and transfer fees when you decide to change brokerage. Instead of paying these fees from your own pocket, you should instead add them to the amount that you paid for a stock when you want to determine the cost basis. When you decide to sell your shares, always subtract the commission from the price of the shares. These costs are considered write-offs because these are expenses that you dealt with directly, expenses that paid for in order to make your money grow. Transaction fees and brokerage fees simply are the money that you have to take out of your own pocket in order to make an investment.

Even though the discount brokerages charge fees that are seemingly lower than others, you should always claim this expense because, like many others, it will cost you in the end. Several fees over the period of a year could add up to hundreds if not thousands of dollars especially if you are a consistent trader who invests in hundreds of dollars each year.

Hold on to stock: People often have a habit of selling their stock when their investments go south. While this is a reasonable move, it could cost you some good money. You see, capital gains of less than a year (short-term) frequently undergo taxation at a higher rate than those of more than a year (long-term). So, what is the tax rate difference between the two?

It could be up to 13 percent and even more in other countries and states and so if you put this into consideration, it would be extremely beneficial to hold on to your stock for more than a year.
When people first get into trading, they plan to participate in equity markets for longer than decades through moving through stock to stock. They plan to do this while still keeping their money working for them actively in the market for the period of their capital accumulation duration. If you are looking to join this crowd, then consider all the tax advantages that come with holding your stock for longer than a year. Your savings could be beyond your expectations.

Conclusion

Thanks for making it through to the end of *Stock Market Investing for Beginners: And Intermediate*, let's hope it was informative and able to provide you with all of the tools you need to achieve your goals, whatever it is that they may be. Just because you've finished this book doesn't mean there is nothing left to learn on the topic, and expanding your horizons is the only way to find the mastery you seek.

Now that you have made it to the end of this book, you hopefully have an understanding of how to successfully move into the second phase of your stock investing career, as well as a strategy or two, or three, that you are anxious to try for the first time. Before you go ahead and start giving it your all, however, it is important that you have realistic expectations as to the level of success you should expect in the near future.

While it is perfectly true that some people experience serious success right out of the gate, it is an unfortunate fact of life that they are the exception rather than the rule. What this means is that you should expect to experience something of a learning curve, especially when you are first figuring out what works for you. This is perfectly normal, however, and if you persevere you will come out the other side better because of it. Instead of getting your hopes up to an unrealistic degree, you should think of your time spent with the stock market as a marathon rather than a sprint which means that slow and steady will win the race every single time.

Finally, if you found this book useful in anyway, a review is always appreciated!

www.ingramcontent.com/pod-product-compliance
Lightning Source LLC
Chambersburg PA
CBHW071434210326
41597CB00020B/3782